EMILY DICKINSON
FACE TO FACE

EMILY DICKINSON
FACE TO FACE

AND

"A HEDGE AWAY"

MARTHA DICKINSON
BIANCHI

WITH A FOREWORD BY

ANTHONY MADRID

McNally Editions

New York

McNally Editions
52 Prince St, New York 10012

Foreword © 2023 by Anthony Madrid

Part I, "Emily Dickinson Face to Face," from *Emily Dickinson Face to Face* by Martha Dickinson Bianchi. Originally published in 1932 by Houghton Mifflin, Boston. Copyright © 1932 by Martha Dickinson Bianchi. Copyright © renewed 1960 by Alfred Leete Hampson. Used by permission of HarperCollins Publishers.

Part II, "A Hedge Away" from *The Life and Letters of Emily Dickinson* by Martha Dickinson Bianchi. Originally published in 1924 by Houghton Mifflin, Boston.

This edition © 2023 by McNally Editions

ISBN: 978-1-946022-58-5
E-book: 978-1-946022-59-2

Designed by Jonathan D. Lippincott

1   3   5   7   9   10   8   6   4   2

CONTENTS

FOREWORD

1

Emily Dickinson Face to Face is a beautiful book. It is judicious, urbane, loving. It was written by a professional novelist in her sixties, a person with a lot of experience evoking and analyzing human personality. She is quite capable of intelligent critical distance on her parents, on Emily Dickinson, and on herself. She comes off like a person of character.

But what makes this little memoir extraordinary, even unique, in all the millions of pages written about Dickinson, is its intimacy. The first page has words to the effect of "My earliest memory of Emily Dickinson was of her opening the door to take us in, on some Sunday when they were dropping us off. She had to babysit us while everybody else went to church. She wouldn't go, so she had to babysit." The year is 1870 or '71. Say the memoirist, later known as Martha Dickinson Bianchi (we'll call her Matty), was four and Emily Dickinson (ED) was forty, that means Matty knew

ED, more or less continuously, through the last fifteen years of ED's life. "Knew"? She probably cuddled with her. Gotta be only six or seven people in the history of the universe who cuddled with Emily Dickinson, and only a couple who give us a child's-eye view of ED with other grown-ups. Here's Matty talking about her mother's judgment of ED's blend of religious faith and skepticism.

> Susan realized that, although Emily took liberties with the Puritan vernacular and dogma when venting her baffled impatience with the Inscrutable, these impish flashes were no more to the underlying God-consciousness of the real Emily than the gargoyle on the roof is to the heart of the Cathedral within.
>
> Whatever my mother's idea of Emily's ultimate recognition may have been, she never suggested her own estimates should be ours. Each one of us for ourselves made our own discovery of her at-homeness with disembodied thought. To come upon her suddenly, looking up into the tops of the trees, as if listening, not to the sounds of common day, not to her own thoughts, but to a mystic inclusion in some higher beauty known only to herself, forbade that we should fully interpret her. Nor was she lacking in a sort of spiritual arrogance—the right of one to whom much is revealed.

Those are stylish sentences, and they go some distance to helping us see how people in Emily's circle *made way* for her. But to me the real takeaway is in that last sentence. It is as thrilling for me to hear someone who knew ED say she was *spiritually arrogant* as it is to watch people in her milieu call her out for being such a weirdo. Which did happen occasionally.

There's a famous bit (a version of it appears in *Face to Face*) where Samuel Bowles arrives from Springfield, and Emily refuses (as she did, more and more, as she got older) to come downstairs. Bowles stands at the foot of the stairs and yells up something like "Emily, you damned rascal! None of your nonsense! Come down at once! I've come all the way from Springfield to see you!" She does descend, and everything is wonderful. But I don't even care that she descended. I'm just glad to hear one of her friends resisting her schtick. She was kind of impossible.

F2F is a treasure because of its golden anecdotes. For example, the thing near the beginning, where Emily and Matty (Matty's a child at the time) are up in Emily's room, listening to the hyper-extended goodbyes being transacted between Lavinia and some group of lady visitors below. Emily's remarks are delicious, something like "Listen to them kissing away down there, Matty. The *traitors!*"

Or there's the wonderful bit, near the end, where Matty shows us at least one of ED's attitudes toward her seclusion:

I remember telling her how, when a child, I once had been sent up to the guest-room to sit quietly by myself as a punishment—until I regretted some trifling dereliction; but I had enjoyed the pretty room so much I had refused to come out when the ban was lifted, and how her [ED's] eyes sparkled as she confided to me, joyously, 'Matty, child, no one could ever punish a Dickinson by shutting her up alone.' And in 1883, when I took her my Shakespeare birthday book for her signature, she highly approved the quotation opposite December 10 [ED's birthday]: 'I hear, yet say not much, but think the more.' (*Henry VI*, Act 4, Sc. 1.)

Her love of being alone up in her room was associated with her feeling for a key, which signified freedom from interruption and the social prevention that beset her downstairs. She would stand looking down, one hand raised, thumb and forefinger closed on an imaginary key, and say, with a quick turn of her wrist, 'It's just a turn—and freedom, Matty!'

Does the above settle the question as to ED's attitude toward her seclusion? It does not. But I love it, all the same. And there are probably thirty bits in *F2F* that are tasty like that. And look how well written it is! "The social prevention that beset her downstairs"—that's like something out of James.

And yet this singular memoir—the first section of a longer book containing a vast pile of letters, notes, and poems to Susan Gilbert Dickinson, Matty's mother—has been out of print almost continually since it was published in 1932. Out of print and very hard to find. It's not quite the kind of text you have to read wearing gloves in the Special Collections room. They have it in the stacks at your local Major Research Library, and you are allowed to eat a muffin while you read it. But obtaining your very own copy was indeed a tricky business, until the present reprint.

To understand why this should have been so, and really to understand why and how *F2F* exists, I'm afraid we must briefly enter a war zone, namely the sulphuric mess that followed ED's death on 15 May 1886. There was all this family nastiness. This little piggy went to market; this little piggy lied in court. This little piggy had a mistress; this one sicced her dogs on the other one's cats. It's hard to keep the characters and the order of operations straight. For one thing, three key players have names that are made out of the same four phonemes, flipped around—viz., Mabel Loomis Todd, Millicent Bingham Todd, Martha Dickinson Bianchi.

But I have spent the last few months in the war zone. I've read most of the key documents on which a person must rely in forming opinions about the personality of Emily Dickinson and the character of her relationships. I've tried hard to extend imaginative sympathy to all the little piggies mentioned above. I had *hoped*, at the beginning of all this, to maintain a kind of lofty objectivity with regard to all the warring factions, but in the end I found myself loyal to Matty. I like her mind. I like her sensibility.

But for now, all tones of warm appreciation and sophisticated lala are about to come to an end, only to be resumed in the mode of fantasy, at the end of this foreword.

2

Summary of the Mess: ED died, and her sister Lavinia found all her papers. Supposedly, Lavinia did not know there were 1,800 poems in that room, had no idea, etc. I'm sure she didn't know there were that many, but she can hardly have been surprised there were a lot.

Controversial question: Did Lavinia have an intelligent appreciation of her sister's literary talent? It's easy to make it look like she did not, but here, as with a great number of controversial points to follow, most of what counts as "evidence" is the testimony of people who despised the person whose mentality we're trying to evaluate. A point to be kept firmly in view.

So, either because Lavinia had some idea of the poems' value, or because she worshiped her sister in a completely empty-headed and despicable way, she wanted the poems to appear in print. Supposedly, she turned to her sister-in-law, Matty's mother, Sue, as the person most qualified to *see* those poems into print.

Controversial question: In what spirit did Lavinia turn to Sue? Was she asking for help from someone she hated? Someone she was physically afraid of? Someone who knew that she, Lavinia, was a friend and comforter to the young woman who was sleeping with her (Sue's) husband—?

At any rate, Sue seems to have accepted the task of seeing the poems into print, but supposedly she did not move expeditiously enough to satisfy Lavinia's sense of urgency. But I don't buy this. I read somewhere (and I believe it) that ED had only been in her grave nine months before the editorial task was handed over, by Lavinia, to Mabel Loomis Todd, the woman who was sleeping with Sue's husband.

Mabel Loomis Todd. I'm going to call her Mabel. She was about to turn thirty when ED died. The affair with Sue's husband (ED's brother, Austin) had been going on for about two and a half years. Mabel's appreciation for ED's poetry, to which Sue introduced her in February 1882 (when everyone in the picture still liked each other), is not much in doubt. Mabel lectured on ED's poetry in the 1890s, and she could supposedly quote reams of it from memory. I believe this.

How did Sue react to the new arrangement? Here, one has to guess, as evidence is lacking. But we do know that Sue had endured a lot over the previous few years. Her eight-year-old son, who was the apple of everyone's eye—including ED's and Austin's—had died not long before Austin and Mabel started having sex. Sue knew about the affair, responded to it exactly as you'd expect. Austin seems to have refused, angrily, to break it off.

Controversial question: Does the Austin-and-Mabel affair deserve any sympathy? It received an immense amount of sympathy from its lead actors, and it has had its eloquent supporters in the years since. I, personally, am medically incapable of liking persons who keep track of their orgasms; just the same, imagining their minds is not impossible for me. They were two people, loaded with sorrows and longing, trying to find their way.

Mabel did not edit the poems alone. She was helped by Thomas Wentworth Higginson, a professional writer and editor who was ED's friend and correspondent for more than twenty years. Since the 1950s, these two early editors have been scolded hundreds of times for not printing the poems exactly as ED wrote them, but (as has been pointed out) literally no one at that time would have printed those poems intact, with their dashes and screwy rhymes and all-over-the-place subjunctive mood. Moreover, if they *had* printed them like that, it is more than probable that the first book of poems (*Poems*, 1890) would have sunk like a stone, and there never would have been another.

The book came out *their* way and was a hit. They put out another. Another hit. Conflicts were brewing with Lavinia. Mabel felt she was doing a ton of work and was being compensated for it at the whim of Her Majesty. Lavinia felt the work was mainly mechanical (just transcribing and cataloging), and that such work did not entitle the clerical worker to any kind of direct nomination in the publisher's contract. The controversial question here is: Was Lavinia being a meanie?

To hear Mabel tell it in the afteryears, Lavinia was an irrational, greedy witch, animated almost entirely by vanity. And maybe she was! But from the unprocessed facts, it's quite possible to see it Lavinia's way, too. The work *was* largely mechanical. And as for the non-mechanical part, picking out a hundred really good poems from a cache of at least a thousand Emily Dickinson lyrics requires no very great penetration or exertion.

Except maybe it does. And *maybe* Mabel was the only person besides Sue who actually "got" Emily. And rewriting lines and finding new rhymes does require judgment and skill.

This is taking too long. Austin died in August 1895, around eight months before *Poems: Third Series* came out. He had promised Mabel a strip of land, but he had failed to actually deed it to her. He had trusted Lavinia (his sister—keep it straight) to take care of it. Why didn't he take care of it himself? Unclear. Why didn't he write out a deposition, as Mabel repeatedly requested, on the subject of what an evil wretch Sue was—? Unclear.

Lavinia, contrary to her desires and better judgment, signed away the land one night. Anyhow, she signed the piece of paper. Later, she claimed the signature was void, because she didn't know what she was signing. There was a court case, open to the public, and apparently much of the Mess was aired. It was child's play to make it look like Mabel was a kind of pirate, shameless and self-serving. Lavinia won her suit; Mabel considered it the upside-down of all justice and reality; and all publication of new ED poems came to a halt for eighteen years (1896–1914).

But where was Matty in all this? Matty was nineteen when ED died. She'd had piano lessons with Mabel, before the Affair. *After* the Affair, after the deaths of her eight-year-old brother and of ED, Matty gained a reputation in some quarters of being stuck-up, pretentious, icy, and hateful. Coincidentally, this xeroxes Sue's reputation, in the exact same quarters. Then Austin (Matty's father—keep it straight) died, and there was the court case, and Matty and Sue started spending a lot more time away from Amherst. They became characters in the very Henry James novels that Matty was later to imitate, learning languages and looking at Europe.

Matty came into her own as a writer in her thirties. She started out as a poet, and had verses printed in high-profile places, like the *Atlantic*. The pieces I've read made no impression on me, but the novels are something else again. These were heavily influenced by *Washington Square* and *Portrait of a Lady* and the like. They are not amateurish books.

More Mess . . . Mabel had published ED's letters, in two volumes, in 1894. That book absolutely excluded Sue as a correspondent, and references to Sue in the letters that *were* printed were removed. References to Austin's courtship of Sue—gone. And so on. This erasure affected the poems, too. A now-famous poem, "One Sister have I in our house— / And one a hedge away . . ." was obliterated, in ink. The only reason we have the poem today is because this wasn't the only copy. And the only reason we have the evidence of the obliteration is because there was a different poem written on the other side of the foolscap, which Austin or Mabel did not dare destroy.

In 1914, Matty entered the *public* fray for the first time. She printed a collection of ED poems that were written to (or at least sent to) Sue. Matty either thought or pretended to think that ED and Sue had been close friends continuously since they were teenagers. Mabel and Co. of course thought this was an outrageous lie. According to them, Emily—like Mabel—had loved Sue before Emily knew what a pitch-black demoness she was. Unfortunately, there existed many short, self-contained notes in ED's handwriting that were inconvenient to this view. For example—

Susan's Idolator keeps a Shrine for Susan.
[*about 1868*]

•

Sue makes sick Days so sweet, we almost hate
our health. Emily—
[*early 1873?*]

•

Only Woman in the World, Accept a Julep—
[*about 1875*]

•

To own a Susan of my own
Is of itself a Bliss—Whatever Realm I forfeit,
Lord, Continue me in this!
[*about 1877*]

•

I must wait a few Days before seeing you—You
are too momentous. But remember it is idolatry,
not indifference.
[*about 1878*]

Such items had to be explained away. (All the dates
are Thomas Johnson's, from the Harvard edition of the
letters.)

Ah, but look what happens. In 1921, Matty published the first biography of ED, as a kind of preface
to a new edition of the letters, one that includes all

the stuff referencing her mother. The text of something like two thirds of the letters was lifted straight out of the 1894 version, without acknowledgment of Mabel's having gathered and edited them. This also happened with several editions of "complete" ED poems, published by Matty over the next fifteen years. The versions from the 1890s, complete with Mabel's and Higginson's interventions, were lifted wholesale, and without credit. By this point, Higginson was dead, so he didn't mind very much. But Mabel was very much alive, as was her daughter, a brilliant and serious person named Millicent . . .

3

I would love to announce that the names of the characters (starting now) have been changed, to protect the Millicent—if only from being confused with the Mabel and the Matty. But I am tied to the facts. My compromise—reducing all these people to their first names—has its own unpleasant side effects, but I'm fighting an impossible situation here. The good news is: In the historical fiction I'm going to propose in a moment, all names could be improved, at will . . .

Indeed, I do see a piece of deep literature (or cinema) waiting to happen here, one that would take the form of a smart dramatization of the Two Daughters. The Matty character should be gentle, artistic, sophisticated, proud. The trauma of her mother's humiliation, etc., must leave her wounded and accidentally wise. But her slowness to strike has to be depicted as WASPy good form and "breeding," not kindness. Millicent, on the other hand, has all the trauma of having been raised by two emotional infants, both of whom were deeply absorbed in their own sexual charisma for years, and didn't much care what the spectacle looked like to their kid. That kid has to be swept up into the public disapprobation, and—crucially—shunned by Matty in childhood.

Now, Millicent, unlike Matty, became an academically trained intellectual (she was the first female awarded a PhD in Geology from Harvard), and more, she eventually came to an explicit reckoning with the ways in which her mother contributed to the Mess. (Late in the game, she read her mother's diaries from the 1890s and almost had a stroke.) But, unlike Matty, she was willing (and more than willing) to attack. She published, in 1945, *Ancestors' Brocades*, an account in 465 pages of the publication *mishegas* from the 1890s, stolidly defending her mother's selfless labor, tarring Sue and Lavinia (especially the latter, because of the notorious lawsuit)—and failing entirely to mention her mother's sexual affair with Austin.

So, in the historical novel, the two daughters do know themselves, but their loyalties to their respective mothers form an insuperable limit to any kind of objective understanding of the whole picture. And here's where we can get kind of arty. Early on, in the book, we can drop a hint that the two women are themselves a clanging "off rhyme," like the ones characteristic of ED's poetry. In real life, both women ran off to Europe and married con men. Matty's guy was some kind of a dashing business cheat, who ran through a bunch of her money (he was Russian but with an Italian name; that's how she got the "Bianchi"). Millicent's was apparently this lying cad who failed to mention he was already married and who told her he had a PhD and I don't know what-all. Matty's adventure took a lot longer to play out than did Millicent's, but that can be tidied up in the novel. Or the movie. The important thing is to show they were intensely at cross purposes all their lives, but in a lot of ways, they were sisters.

Much, much could be done in a movie, by playing peek-a-boo with the ED character. The movie isn't about her, so she can be confined to flashbacks, where she is allowed to speak through a half-open door, like she really did. Matty's immense privilege of seeing ED face to face should be handled very chastely. The book you're holding in your hands will supply all the material for that.

A great deal more could be said here. It is my considered opinion that no life comparably documented has ever in the history of the human race had more constructions foisted upon it than ED's. I'm not even going to go into the stuff that's on TV right now. The only thing to do, if you want to weigh in on ED's "deal" with any of the people in this picture, the three *M*s, the sibs, the neighbors, the friends—especially Higginson and supremely Sue—is to read and digest the triple-decker version of ED's letters (Harvard, 1958). You will see: the *tone* of countless sentences is hopelessly ambiguous. This is why all biographies of ED relentlessly do that thing that gets you scolded in an MFA fiction workshop— namely, lines of dialogue followed by "she grumbled sarcastically" and the like.

F2F remains. It, too, is a construction. But it has the authority that its title implies. The only other book like it—i.e., a real memoir by an eye witness—is the truly un-gettable *Emily Dickinson Friend and Neighbor*, by MacGregor Jenkins. I read it online. Although it is informative, it is ramjam with trite flummery—just nothing, compared to *F2F*.

But never mind that, for now. Never mind the Mess. Just give Matty a couple hours, and then I need you to think seriously about the Two Daughters Project. For the task of "injecting some integrity into the Dickinson controversy" remains to be done.

Anthony Madrid
Victoria, Texas, 2022

NOTE ON THE TEXT

Emily Dickinson Face to Face: Unpublished Letters with Notes and Reminiscences, by her niece Martha Dickinson Bianchi, with a foreword by Alfred Leete Hampson, was originally published in 1932 by Houghton Mifflin. The book was 291 pages long and included photographic images, facsimiles, and an index. The last section of the book proper, containing ninety-six pages, is called "Letters and Notes of Emily Dickinson." That part of the book probably accounts for at least half of Matty's motivation in going to press, but it is not included here. What follows is only the first section of the book (sixty-eight pages long, in the original), conveniently entitled "Emily Dickinson Face to Face." The section is self-contained; separating it from the other parts does it no harm.

We have included, as an appendix, the personal recollections that Matty published under the title "A Hedge Away" in *The Life and Letters of Emily Dickinson*

(Houghton Mifflin, 1924), fourteen pages in the original. It should also be noted that Matty had already used the "hedge" concept in the title of her first book of poetry (*Within the Hedge*, 1899). But of course, in the present case, it alludes to the suppressed poem mentioned on page xvii of the foreword.

That famous line of bushes, which formed the border of ED's physical world during all the time Matty knew her, held great significance for the writer known to us as Martha Gilbert Dickinson Bianchi. Her titles were designed to underscore the difference between Outsiders and Inhabitants: persons whose fantasies were based on surmise, versus those whose fantasies were based on contact.

I
EMILY DICKINSON
FACE TO FACE

My first definite memory of my Aunt Emily is of her coming to the door to meet me in her white dress—looking to me just like another little girl—when I was to be left with her for safe-keeping on Sunday mornings while the grown-ups of both households went to church.

My Aunt Lavinia's cats—Tabby, Drummy-doodles, Buffy, and Tootsie—sat about the kitchen with an eye half open for trouble. On week-days their purr power invited investigation—as far as teeth and claws allowed; but on Sunday mornings they were safe. I had Aunt Emily. On regular days she was quicksilver. On Sunday, by some divine law of the holy day, she was mine.

First of all she let me water her plants in her little conservatory—cape jasmine, heliotrope, and ferns—reaching up to the higher shelves by a tiny watering-pot with a long, slender spout like the antennæ of insects, which had been made for her after an idea of her father's. Whatever it was we were doing, she was intent upon it—taking it seriously or making fun of it all. I had only to look up into her eyes to be sure she was having just as good a time 'playing together' as I was. And to me it was enchantment.

In summer we watched the orioles outside—or the cherries ripening—or the bees—or a random humming-bird at the honeysuckle by the east window where her little writing-table stood; for in Aunt Emily's time there were three tall cherry trees in a line just bordering the flagstone walk at the east side of the house, and all the way down to the garden plum and pear trees, very white and garlandly in the spring. Where the slope in the grass came, to the lower terrace, the orchard began, with apple blossoms for Whit-Sunday, which we called 'White-Sunday,' being 'dissenters.'[1] But this is all changed now, and the wild flowers in the long grass, violets and 'innocents' and their kind, have long since given way to lawn and lawnmower, unknown when she dwelt there. There was a picket fence outside the high hemlock hedge, with a driveway gate and two smaller gates similar in design to those still standing in front of our own house. All three were kept closed. To leave one open was a misdemeanor on our part or that of the guilty caller or errand boy. No trolley line then marred the country road.[2]

---

1 When we forgot, my father brought us up short with 'If you mean *White*-Sunday, say so!'

2 No photograph of the home of Emily Dickinson showing trolley poles and tracks and electric light poles and wires could have been taken during her lifetime, as the first electricity for lighting purposes was not intro-duced into Amherst until 1893 (*History of Amherst*), seven years after my

It was a softer, more sequestered effect altogether before Amherst became modernized and what was called 'up-to-date' by those who revolutionized it. How shall one instill the atmosphere within that green hedge so that the inquisitive outsider of today catches the retiring seclusion of it as it was then?

About a certain time on these Sunday mornings we always went downstairs to the deep hoardingcellar, past the locked stone wine-cellar where the sweet Malmsey wine was kept that 'Grandma' liked to offer her genteelest lady callers of an afternoon—and the old rye and sherry and port waiting for 'Grandpa's' juridical guests. At the south, between two narrow grated windows on a level with the front walk, was Aunt Emily's own cupboard, where she kept the rich, dark gingerbread that Aunt Lavinia, with compunctions for our digestion, said was 'too rich for children.' We children knew, of course, that it was because Aunt Lavinia wanted it all for herself. It was my brother Ned who once was carried home screaming: 'I *won't* have a caraway cookie! I *will* see my Aunt Emily! I *will* have a *Rich*!'

To us as well as to the little band of marauding confederates, 'Did' and 'Mac' Jenkins and the three Mather children, Aunt Emily stood for *indulgence.* However the Powers of both houses ruled to put down piracy on the high seas or revolution in the back yard, she held a mandate for us. No matter when the family came back for me

aunt's death, and the street railway not until 1896. (Franchise for street railway on Main Street granted May 23, 1896. *Town Records.*)

from church, it was always too soon, and her voice when she cried, 'Matty, they are *here*!' was as if the Indians were attacking!

At the end of one of these unforgettable mornings—when I couldn't have been more than six—Aunt Emily taught me the precocious psychology of 'treason, stratagem and spoils'—not in words, of course, just an inkling of their meaning—when she asked me, in her most beguiling tone, 'Would Matty like to have a pussy of her own to take home and keep always?'—adding with a catch in her breath—as their lawful owner was upon us—'Take more than one! Take them all! Don't stop to choose, dear!' Then a door closed behind her. I had lost her again. It was treason not to love the pussies. It was stratagem to dispose of them when Aunt Lavinia was in church. The spoils were stolen kittens—or would have been if Aunt Lavinia had not come home just when she did. No, Aunt Emily never appreciated cats. They were always getting under her feet as she carried precious tea-cups in or out, or delicate concoctions of her own, often causing a slip, a smash, a day of reckoning. She was sated with them from their kittenhood up.

The unconscious psychology of all my various feelings about Aunt Emily as a child was summed up when, avenging myself upon a small neighbor for some wrong, I cried with all the scorn I could command: 'Anyway—*you* haven't got an Aunt Emily! Your aunts are just common ant-heap ants!'

I can remember just one of my grandfather's Commencement tea-parties, probably the last of those Amherst 'social classics.' I passed the teaspoons on a tiny silver tray, following the man with the coffee cups—sugar and cream being entrusted to older hands. I remember Aunt Emily standing by the east window in the dining-room, where the more intimate guests came to find her and take a glass of sherry poured from the great glass decanter with her own deft hand. The same decanters and thin old silver spoons with baskets of flowers on the handles, the engraved oblong silver tray, are now in my possession, with the rest of the family treasures.

The next definite memory of the part Aunt Emily played in our lives is one of cold December twilights— the library fire of birch wood from the Pelham hillside blazing on the hearth—and out on the snow in the rhododendron bed as well, by some magic we could never understand—while 'Sister Sue' (my mother) with her children waited for their father to come home to supper. Then across the yard came Timothy, the man-of-all-work, bringing over the milk, the shadow of his legs as he walked swinging his lantern, now long—now short— slanting with each step in dancing curves over the snow. He always carried the foaming pails into the kitchen at the old house first, before bringing our share, which gave Aunt Emily a chance to use him as her nightly messenger.

We would watch him, fascinated, until our mother suggested, 'Which one of you children wants to run out and meet Tim and see if Aunt Emily sent anything over tonight?' That always started a race to the kitchen to see who could be the first to get the message.

Oftenest it was a cardboard box, and Tim said, as we took it from him, 'From Miss Im'ly.'

In it would be perhaps three tiny frosted, heart-shaped cakes, or some of her chocolate caramels—with a flower on top, heliotrope, a red lily, or cape jasmine— and underneath always a note or a poem for our mother. We always waited for her to read it to us, feeling very important to be included and fascinated by the sound of the words before we were old enough to grasp their meaning. Some of these notes are the brief messages that were afterward published as 'The Single Hound.'

Another memory, when I was still very young, is of a summer afternoon in the wide, old, upper hall of the Mansion with Aunt Emily while some 'lady-callers' were taking protracted leave of my Aunt Lavinia below. The front door stood invitingly open—but still more fond partings kept coming up to us. Aunt Emily stood beside me, looking down on the scene, finger on lip. 'Matty, child, hear them kiss!—the traitors!' And later came over, addressed to me—a typically Aunt Emily perfor-mance, recognizing me as her accomplice, though, of course, intended for my mother—her delicious perpet-uation of it, the poem—

> The leaves, like women, interchange
>   Sagacious confidence;

Somewhat of nods, and somewhat of
Portentous inference,

The parties in both cases
Enjoining secrecy—
Inviolable compact
To notoriety.

Her stage whisper, her gesture, can never be lost to
my memory of her. For us all her greatest charm was
her taking us as equals in age, conspiracy, and cynicism.
Later I knew better what she meant; she was not in the
least aspersing her sex, but shrewdly rating the feline
gift at summer afternoon relations in a country town
where gossip was scarce and highly prized accordingly.

That upper hall was my happiest hunting ground—
Aunt Emily's room opened from it, and it was beyond
the long arm of kitchen authority. From the very earliest
time I can remember anything, I went in and out of
her room at all ages, and never was there a picture of
George Gould on the walls.[3] An open Franklin stove
made a pretty blaze in cold weather, and a little writing-
table at which I was allowed to scribble imaginary notes
before I knew my letters stood by a south window. A sort
of lookout, too, it had become, from which she could
'observe the earth beneath.'

Once, in my early teens, when I was there with her,
the front-door bell jangled under us, and, spying down

---

3 This contradicts a recent unfounded suggestion to the contrary.

upon a stranger sent to call upon her by some mutual friend, Aunt Emily dismissed him unreceived after one glance from her window, remarking, 'His face is as handsome and as meaningless as the full moon.'

Again she called me to come and peep at a new Professor recently come to the college, saying, 'Look, dear, his face is as pretty as a cloth pink!'—her mouth curling in sheer fun as she uttered it and one hand motioning as if to throw him away. Any flash of characterization from her was unforgettable.

Of course, Aunt Emily already had become selective, to say the least, in those she chose to receive; but no one ever was known to fail a welcome from Aunt Lavinia, her vicarious representative. Her bland hospitality to callers, as to plain sewing-women, berry-vendors, people who wanted flowers and always got them for funerals or weddings or some girl going to a 'ball' and lacking a bouquet, never failed. However grotesque the interruption, her suavity persevered.

I remember once overhearing a glib voice at the door enquiring—with intent to sell some sort of panacea—'Have you cockroaches, rats or mice, water-bugs, beetles or ——' when Aunt Lavinia broke in with an assuring smile, 'No, we have not; but I don't think I will take any this morning, thank you.'

My sharpest recollection of my grandfather[4] is of him standing in our dining-room door at breakfast-time, as he had a habit of stopping in on his way to the office—to walk up with my father.

4 Emily Dickinson's father.

On one especial morning I found him very much in the way of my own transit around the table with a new tin train of cars.

'Get out of the way there, Mister G'andpa!' I warned, with an utter lack of fear or respect that so warmed his heart that he took out his wallet and handed me twenty-five cents in scrip such as was in use for some years after the Civil War. It was the first large sum of money I had ever had of my own. And when Thanksgiving came around, he insisted I should be brought over to the family dinner, where, perched on his fattest dictionary, I sat at the table and was allowed my first taste of turkey and mince pie.

Thanksgiving day was the favorite festival of them all. There was never a Thanksgiving dinner in the house after his death, and the Commencement teaparties were no more. All that part of their life went with him, its ruling spirit.

I remember my grandfather's funeral by the odor of syringa, and the excitement of settees from College Hall placed in rows on the front lawn to accommodate those the house could not hold, but most of all by my terror at my father's grief. The world seemed coming to an end. And where was Aunt Emily? Why did she not sit in the library with the family if he could? She stayed upstairs in her own room with the door open just a crack, where she could hear without being seen. I could not get to her because there were so many strangers sitting in thick rows between us, filling the hall.

Among my early memories of my grandmother[5] is of her always enquiring if I had learned to sew yet, and if I had got a thimble. Her hopes for my accomplishments were apt to be embarrassing. I see her still in a dainty lavender morning dress with the sunshine on her curling white hair, standing at the end of the piazza to watch my grandfather drive away to Court at Northampton. She would be a little anxious about him until he was safely back, as she could never help being when any of her loved ones were ever so briefly away from her care. Her face was a little clouded as she turned away to watch Maggie at the yellow churn—for no butter was ever good enough but their own with each pat decorated with the image of a cow, a work of art in its way; or set off to tend a sick neighbor, or whatever the morning duty lay nearest her hands so seldom idle. Gentleness was her 'strong enforcement' in that rather eruptive environment of hers. Unconsciously each one depended on her calming influence.

A year after my grandfather's death she was paralyzed, and after that I was sent over on Sunday afternoons to carry some dainty 'with Mamma's love,' and this weekly visit was as unescapable as it was frightening to me—as to any healthy child. The window shades were two thirds down, which made everything seem solemn, and the room had a vague odor of roses and camphor. My grandmother lay very flat, her white curls spread out on the pillow, looking like a beautiful wax

---

5 Emily Dickinson's mother.

doll, I thought. What if she should die while I was there?

Aunt Emily was my rescuer. She must have known a child's helpless feelings about sick people as she beckoned me from the door at the head of the bed, where she was invisible to the occupant.

There was no greater delight than to watch Aunt Emily cook—'helping' her she called it. She was rather *précieuse* about it—using silver to stir with and glass to measure by. Her utensils were private, those exquisite moulds from which her wine-jelly slipped trembling without a blemish in the pattern of a rose or sheaf of wheat; and the round bread pans she used to ensure crust in baking her father's 'daily bread' for which he asked each morning at Family Prayers. An imaginary line was drawn about all her 'properties' which seemed to protect them against alien fingers—lent a difference in taste to the results she produced. Her technique was as precise as that of a musician playing scales. She never trusted to her imagination there—never gave herself a chance to get a quarter of a teaspoonful of Eternity in by mistake, as she gravely explained, though I caught a twinkle in her eyes, when she was concocting that wine-flavored delight she called 'Homestead Charlotte Russe.'

And since there is no portrait of her as I knew her, in her maturity, let me say that she was of medium height, decisive in manner, not frail nor ever suggestive of ill health. Colonel Higginson[6] has said she had not

---

6 It has been pointed out that Colonel Higginson's letter, written to his wife directly after his first and only meeting with Aunt Emily, will

a single good feature, but neither had she a single bad one, and her dark, expressive eyes with their tint of bronze, and Titian hair set off by her white skin, were always considered remarkable by others. Indeed, the richness of her hair and eyes were her salient points, oftenest commented on. She had regular features, and her upper lip, a trifle long, gave her face a slightly ascetic expression. In their youth the furbelows and frills of girlhood were dear to both the aunts, as Aunt Lavinia's diary repeatedly attests as well as Aunt Emily's letters to my mother and others. For 'best' they wore gay muslins in summer and bright merinos in winter; their new bonnets and shawls were events to date by. They had a good deal of old-fashioned jewelry, some of it originally their mother's, and in addition to their girlish trinkets were garnet brooches and sleeve-buttons and various heavy gold bracelets. Some foreign corals and cameos—very much in vogue then—were brought them from abroad by a returning friend of their parents; also elaborate breastpins of mosaic rimmed in gold—'very elegant' in the eyes of their girlfriends. Aunt Lavinia continued to wear hers on occasions, but in my day Aunt Emily wore only a white-and-gold cameo pin at her throat to hold the dainty niching that invariably finished the neck of her white dresses, and sometimes her gold watch tucked in her belt, a ring or two; and the rest was put away in velvet-lined boxes, except as it was brought out, on

---

seem to give to many a clearer impression than his later recollections published years afterward.

rare occasions at my request, to be seen and admired. During my memory of her she wore white exclusively, and when the season turned chill, a little shoulder cape crocheted of soft white worsted and run through with a ribbon, and over her hair a brown velvet net or snood. She often moved about in a sort of revery of her own— flitting always—and quick as a trout if disturbed. Her low-pitched voice was the instrument of an unconscious artist, almost husky at times of intensity, sweetly confidential, exciting in moments of extravaganza or 'outrage,' satiric, sympathetic, breathless in turn. Colonel Higginson mentioned her soft voice, as well as her more familiar friends, and even callers at the house who never saw her, but overheard her messages, still speak of it.[7]

---

7 In response to the request of Colonel Higginson for a likeness of herself, Aunt Emily wrote in 1862: 'Could you believe me without? I had no portrait now . . . It often alarms father. He says death might occur, and he has moulds of all the rest, but has no mould of me; but I noticed the quick wore off those things in a few days, and forestall the dishonor.' Thus did Emily Dickinson repudiate any picture of herself at that time. This lack of any satisfactory likeness led Aunt Lavinia in the nineties to permit the publication one taken from a childhood group, but the inadequacy of this became a constant source of regret to her, as she felt the child face insufficiently indicated the later Emily Dickinson of the *Poems*. Consequently, Aunt Lavinia gave explicit directions that in future editions— should a portrait be required—a miniature made by her direction from a photograph of an old daguerreotype should be used as the best means of suggesting the appearance of her sister as she was known by her contemporaries. This miniature she felt gave a far truer impression than anything else available, especially in regard to the arrangement of the hair, which, not only according to the family memory, but also as has been described in a letter written by Aunt Emily's contemporary and friend, Emily Fowler Ford, lay in auburn rings all over her head, and was customarily worn parted low on her brow, drooping loosely in thick strands to a coil at the back of her neck. (In my day it retained its rather wavy, clustering tendency,

The wide kitchen spread across the back of the house from east to west. There were two windows on the west and two more in the big pantry opening from it, as well as another window on the east, and a door opening on a side porch which was never shut except on account of the weather. At the back was a big scullery, where all but the actual cooking went on unseen. The walls were painted a light green and the doors and window-casings a deep yellow. The range was an ornamental adjunct, built into the wall. Altogether the kitchen was a cheerful and much-frequented quarter—the arena of much-varied family event. The sun touched it with a final beam too—beneath the dark pine trees—

---

and was partly covered by a velvet net or snood, but never flattened down or strained back.) Aunt Lavinia kept this miniature by her and showed it to her friends with pride and satisfaction, saying, 'Emily has come back to me.' I never saw, either in my grandfather's or my father's house, any portrait of my Aunt Emily Dickinson other than these two, the originals of both being in my possession. In view, therefore, of Aunt Emily's repudiation of any former picture and of Aunt Lavinia's delight in this one, the miniature was included in the *Life and Letters* at the request of the publishers and in accordance with Aunt Lavinia's positive directions, accompanied by an explicit statement of its origin. It was later, by the courtesy of Houghton Mifflin Company, lent to Little, Brown and Company. I am indebted to Miss Gertrude Graves for telling me, during the summer of 1931, the story of the miniature and her own part in it, which she gladly gave me permission to publish. She said it was during a visit to the Graves's home in the autumn of 1896 (the year after my father's death) that Aunt Lavinia expressed her longing for a portrait of her sister Emily, and eventually put the whole matter in her hands. Aunt Lavinia's directions were followed in detail, and through the gracious assistance of Miss Laura Hills, the miniature painter, the result was so satisfactory that it gave Aunt Lavinia the greatest happiness, so that she wrote Miss Graves the words she always reiterated concerning it—'Emily has come back to me!'.

Blazing in gold and quenching in purple,
  Leaping like leopards to the sky,
Then at the feet of the old horizon
  Laying her spotted face, to die;

Stooping as low as the kitchen window,
  Touching the roof and tinting the barn,
Kissing her bonnet to the meadow—
  And the juggler of day is gone![8]

Here the supremacy which was ours at brief inter-
vals was rightly that of Maggie in calico—described
by Aunt Emily as 'sensational in temperament.' Timothy, the 'hired man,' an ex-sailor with blue stars and
anchors tattooed on his mighty arms, had his exits
and entrances.

No matter what the name of the 'hired man,' he was
always 'Miss Im'ly's' slave.' Never a workman on the place
but conspired for her. The peerage of the early Irish in
Amherst could be cited in the list of those who boy and
man at one time or another served 'the old Squire.' Aunt
Emily trusted them with her errands of what she named 'a
confidential nature'—flower or fruit or some dainty made
by herself, not intended for home consumption—on their
way home after their day's work. Not one of them but
would trudge an extra half-mile and tell her it was right
on his way, in response to her gentle 'Dennis, would you

---

8 *Poems of Emily Dickinson*, Centenary Edition, Little, Brown and
Company, p. 88.

be too tired———?' 'Pat, would it be too much out of your way———?'

Nevertheless, it was Aunt Lavinia who stood by them and did for them practically when their families were sick or in trouble, going herself to make sure all was being done, and attending to the necessary supplies. She had what the French call 'of the character,' as was sensed by them all in their own terms. To us, however, it was a convincing example of the power of personality over practicality that, while they respected and depended on Aunt Lavinia, they went right on giving their allegiance to Aunt Emily.

Amusing and witty as she was capable, Aunt Lavinia was a great 'wag' at times, and when she was in that vein no one reveled in her gift for reproducing the local scene and those who acted in it more than Aunt Emily. I have often heard Aunt Lavinia, for our benefit 'take off' with dramatic exaggeration—and meaning glances to point the difference in manners obtaining in their day—the comedy of the mock panic in the house of long ago when the Squire came home to dinner at noon. According to her, at their mother's suggestion—'Girls, your father is coming!'—they did not let the telltale ends of their lives stick out. Emily would vanish into the front hall, their mother peer about to be sure nothing was amiss—no cat in a forbidden chair, the morning newspaper folded and in its place—no omission to disturb her approaching husband, weary from his long summer morning of work at his law office, looking for peace and rest in his orderly home. He would find her noting the thermometer in the east window—she would be able to tell him exactly where the mercury stood, if he expressed any interest to know.

Lavinia, herself, dispersing too glaring disorders as she sped, would be already at the side door to take his hat, a glossy beaver hat, and his cane, a gold-headed cane. For even though the Squire passed down an empty street, by the Sweetsers' cows pastured on his left and reached no habitation until his son's, the silk hat and gold cane were the indispensable adjuncts of his like in the eighteen-sixties. Let there be no compromise of the decent formalities, even if it was midsummer and torrid high noon at that, with the cicadas singing away in the trees like the voices of lightning.

But whenever their father came home, the event was of a definite momentousness. He was not aware, of course, that the calm so devotedly evoked into which he walked was often fictitious—that a few moments before his hand was upon the gate the berry-kettle had boiled over onto the stove, the yellow cat had had a fit, someone had fallen downstairs, or any other of the hundred possible household crises had been in full swing. No matter what the calamity, no matter how stark the domestic emergency, by the time he reached the side piazza the peace of Heaven's own morn lay thick upon the atmosphere. The old New England worship of the 'Head of the House' here prevailed in every nerve—was nowhere more exquisitely demonstrated.

Though their father was formal by nature, his heart was as warm as his manner was cold. Abrupt, shy of all sentiment in exhibition, wholly devoted to his hearth and family, it would have amazed him to know his daily coming cast even so fond a shadow before him.

'Don't worry your father! Don't trouble your father with it!'—was their mother's repeated, loving admonition.

Aunt Lavinia said her summer frocks, for example, sometimes worried 'Father' when she wore them in the fashion of the day well cut down on the shoulder (hers, it seems, being uncommonly white and pretty shoulders). And her manner was rather languishing, too, which occasionally brought down on her 'Father's' stiff rebuke: 'Lavinia, don't be so affected! Put on a shawl!'—which, my mother said, his pretty younger daughter did with a pout that made her prettier than ever.

The house being brick and kept sacredly closed was always cool with a peculiar chill as one went into it from the hot sun outside. The dining-room carried the scent of the twin honeysuckle in the great glass pitcher on the dining-table. The old mahogany sideboard, brought with my grandmother's wedding dower, uphill and down dale, by brindle ox power, was covered with old blue china. The Franklin pitcher stood there, and the copper glaze on the shelf above. From the fabulous soup tureen stuck out a few of 'Father's' most important papers—put there for safe-keeping. There was asparagus fern in the open Franklin stove where in winter a bright blaze leapt up.

The table was laid for four. Old Hannah,[9] a woman servant long before Maggie's time, so large that Emily said she 'moved about in a calico sarcophagus,' stood waiting for the family to sit down. Lavinia was ready with the soothing extenuation should it prove useful. The scene, as related, closes with their mother smiling a trifle apprehensively, but wholly blest and honored by her state and calling, as 'Father' seated himself and listened approvingly to her gentle statement: 'The mercury stands at seventy-eight. Should you have thought it so warm, Edward—or warmer?'—affecting not to hear Emily's comment in a piercing whisper of disrespect, 'Providence ought to be above it!'—lest he did what he ought and reproved her—Emily—whom he never reproved, and whom he never thwarted even later on—when the chosen solitude of his brilliant daughter must have been a blow to his worldly pride.

9 The later servant, Maggie, did not come into the service of the family until the late sixties. In addition to 'Margaret,' the wife of Richard (or 'Dick'), a man who worked on the place, Aunt Emily mentions their predecessor, this old Hannah, in a note to my mother: 'Neddy is safe. Just serenaded Hannah, and is running off with a corn-leaf tail, looking back for cheers.' And Neddie's own nurse, Mary Casey, stated at Amherst, during a call made on the occasion of the Massachusetts Tercentenary Celebration in 1930, that she herself was with our family until 1867, and that Maggie Mahar was not in service at the 'Mansion' at that time. Aunt Emily's first mention of Maggie occurs in 1869, thus making an anachronism of an anonymous tale recently published, that following upon the graduation and departure of George Gould from Amherst in 1850, Deacon Luke Sweetser carried letters from him to the servant Maggie, to be given to Aunt Emily in defiance of her father's alleged wishes that all communication be cut off—to say nothing of the moral anachronism of supposing a Deacon, so renowned for his piety and sanctity, guilty of the willful deception of his lifelong friend and nearest neighbor, by secretly conveying forbidden love-letters to his daughter with the aid of an Irish servant.

The 'Northwest Passage' was so named by Emily and 'Sister Sue.'[10] It lay between the kitchen and the middle hall which led to that exclusive 'front part' where the elders alone roamed at will. It was lighted by a glass door at one end, and offered access or escape equally in five directions, including that of the dark middle stairway— for the old house has three in all. This one we children called 'the secret stairway,' and associated its possibilities with exciting stories of Indians in old Hadley. When the door into the china closet was open—where the best white-and-gold china was stored high above profane reach on red painted shelves—the mystery dwindled; but it was a likely place to catch up with Aunt Emily for young or old.

Here these two allies often met—as Aunt Emily from her window, seeing my mother coming across the lawn, hurried down to meet her, hoping for a few words about her latest poem sent over to her, before the family interrupted with a more general welcome.

---

10 The 'Northwest Passage' got its name from the northwest passage by sea between the Atlantic and Pacific Oceans long vainly sought. Just how it was derived in this instance is easy for the initiated to fancy. That others outside the family recall it as part of the household matter-of-course has been charmingly retold this summer (1931) in a note from Mrs. Annie Holland Howe (Mrs. John K. Howe), the older daughter of Dr. J. G. Holland, who wrote me: 'When I was a young girl visiting in Amherst, I went to a reception in your grandparents' house, and met your Aunt Emily. She was so surrounded by people that I had no chance to talk with her, and she asked me to call on her the next morning. She received me in a little back hall that connected with the kitchen. It was dimly lighted. She asked if I would have a glass of wine or a rose. I told her I would take the rose, and she went to the garden and brought one in to me. She seemed very unusual, and her voice, her looks, and her whole personality made an impression on me that is still very vivid after all these years.'

'Are you sure we are making the most of it, Sue?'

'Any advices, Emily? If a man die shall he live again?'—a hurried greeting, then the discussion of the subject in hand—what each acclaimed or condemned—for soon the door of the dining-room would be cracking open and my grandmother would chide: 'Why, Emily, don't keep Sue standing in the hall! Come right in, Sue. Have you heard the particulars of——?' the recentest birth, death, default in social integrity. Or Aunt Lavinia's voice from the top of the stairs: 'Take Sue into the dining-room, Emily. The fire is bright there. Don't keep her in the draught, she will take cold. I'll be right down.' And how, pray, were they to talk of poetry with the family alert to give and take the latest news of village or family?

It was here that my mother, who—though knowing Aunt Emily's aversion to having her verses printed had yielded to Mr. Bowles's[11] repeated requests and let the *Republican* have her lines about the snake beginning:

> A narrow fellow in the grass
> Occasionally rides;

gave the paper to Aunt Emily, and watched hopefully yet fearfully for the result of her own temerity. And Emily took it absent-mindedly in her hand, without glance or comment, and on the familiar phenomena of the opening door and voice from above—*was not.*

---

11 Samuel Bowles, editor of the *Springfield Republican.*

'Uncle Sam' Bowles was urgent for more. The third verse amused him most:

> He likes a boggy acre,
> A floor too cool for corn.
> Yet when a child, and barefoot,
> I more than once at morn,
>
> Have passed, I thought, a whip-lash, etc.

'How did that girl ever know that a boggy field wasn't good for corn?' he demanded of 'Sister Sue,' holding Emily guiltless of farming lore.

'Oh, you forget that was Emily "*when a boy*"!' was the reply. But she never repeated the experiment, referring him always to Emily.

There can be no doubt of Aunt Emily's disinclination to see herself out in the world in print, when one recalls Helen Hunt's fruitless urging and 'Uncle Sam's' eagerness to open the doors to her. If she really wanted publicity, it was hers for the accepting, but she declared, publication is as 'foreign to my thought as firmament to fin'; and again,

> Publication is the auction
> Of the mind of man—

admitting that poverty may justify it, but setting it outside her personal pale with finality.

It was here that Sue gave Emily the fantastic and unique story of the Indian Devil by Harriet Prescott Spofford, called 'Circumstance,' which had just appeared in the *Atlantic Monthly*—and here that Emily gave it back, saying: 'Sue, it is the only thing I ever read in my life that I didn't think I could have imagined myself!'

Later came these two lines—'You stand nearer the world than I do, Susan. Send me everything she writes.' And the selfsame early *Atlantic*s of Sue's sent in response are still extant.

After one of these brief meetings there would often come over one of Aunt Emily's most arresting and individual notes, inspired by their mood. Many of those included in the final chapter of this volume were of such origin—the sentences she had no time to say before the family claimed Sue and her budget of local information.

Sometimes they exchanged a mere quip clipped for each other at random for its significance or sheer drollery. For 'droll' was one of Aunt Emily's most constant words.

Among these, preserved by my mother, was the following:

Talleyrand, on the death of a certain Marquis with whose wife he had enjoyed relations, intimate but impermanent, wrote in consolation upon his death—

Chère Marquise,

Helas!

TALLEYRAND.

There is also a leaf from a daily Shakespeare calendar: 'When most I wink, then do my eyes best see, for all the day they view things unrespected.' Examples of this—Loyola, Madame Beck, Emily. (In my mother's handwriting.)

Another cutting, sent to her by Emily, was this:

> While our home is here
> No sounding name is half so dear;
> When fades at length our lingering day
> Who cares what pompous tombstones say?
> Read on the hearts that love us still—
> Hic jacet Joe. Hic jacet Bill.

In this same refuge of swiftly threatened privacy, my mother spoke to Emily of her poem, also published without permission, included by Helen Hunt in the 'Masque of Poets,' and saw her go so white she regretted the impulse which had led her to express her own thrill in it.

From the time when it was just part of some childhood game—played with or without the wandering horde of hungry little neighbors who went to Aunt Emily for forbidden cake between meals—to the older years when I, too, wanted to see her for my own varying reasons, my favorite approach was by signal at her window. That west window of hers!—even when we were grown up how we all passed it 'looking back for cheers' and continued to regard it as the stage-box overlooking our personal drama! If her response was favoring, I hurried through the kitchen without let or hindrance from anybody on my way to my own chance to see her alone in the Northwest Passage. 'Want to see you without witnesses!' was a message hailed by each one of us alike. It meant something she had for us—or something she was saving to tell us.

No one ever valued or fostered the fascination of a secret for a child as she did. When she wrote of my younger brother, 'Gilbert rejoiced in secrets. His young life was panting with them,' it was just as true of his Aunt Emily. She lent a contraband thrill to the slightest pretext.

It was in one of these delicious moments by ourselves that I dared to ask her whether she loved my father or Aunt Lavinia best. 'Both—*best*,' she assured me gravely, stressing the word best.

It was here, when 'Did' Jenkins and I set out to print in our own hand a little neighborhood newspaper, we consulted Aunt Emily as to the name. She thought a minute, then answered decidedly, 'The Fortnightly Bumble Bee,' promising us not only her subscription for all time, but contributions. Only one copy was issued from our playroom, which—alas!—has gone 'down the back entry of time' carrying that precious Emily 'local' with it.

It was here also, by the time I was sixteen, I would tell her about the party of the night before, in which she never forgot to be interested—informal little affairs they were, with a few college boys asked in, and dancing as long as any of the girls would play the piano to keep the music going.

'Did you love the party, dear?' she would ask, to set me off; and once, when I failed to enthuse, she nodded shrewdly as she explained the trouble to me—'I see, Coroner's verdict—*Dead!*'—a phrase for a dull person or party that was never to fall into disuse in our intimate circle.

Sacred little Northwest Passage! From my farthest memory it is more associated with the deathless impression of Aunt Emily than any of the dignified rooms in that stately house.

This had been the place where she had chosen to renew her broken life after the funeral of my grandfather, when the inevitable routine of the household closed in upon her again and she dropped back into her daily round—seeing us briefly in transit—with a few choking words at first, her tears uncontrollable, her faith in life broken; her grief less violent in expression than Aunt Lavinia's, less grim than my father's—but all as one in their sudden destitution.[12]

Of course by the time I had grown up enough really to know Aunt Emily, both the 'Elizabeth' of baptism and the 'Emilie' of her young fancy had been shed. She was Emily Dickinson. The superfluous dropped from her as her habit of thought strengthened.

---

12 Emily's father was stricken with apoplexy while making a speech before the Legislature at Boston in 1874.

Our generation had stolen a march on the calendar, and even in the late seventies and early eighties had begun to slip over the rim of the next century from hers. Through this universal tendency, illustrated for her in us, she caught an idea of a new order of life as lived by young people taking outdoor sports, dancing, and even 'playing cards' as a matter of course—a spectacle no less startling in contrast to her own upbringing than the present time to our own. To every aspect of this she lent herself curiously. While I was a little girl she had always revelled in my hats with 'dare-devil bows,' and some 'stratified stockings' which were red with white stripes— much in vogue among my playmates—and which had once caused the pompous Judge Lord to enquire if I was 'intended for a tonsorial advertisement'; and the more sophisticated wardrobe of my advancing teens diverted her not a little in contrast to her own.

'I in fustian,' she would profess, noting the comparison by lifting a sash-fringe with a mock timid finger, or touching one of my modish sleeves with exaggerated respect. Most of all her 'vote' was for my highest-heeled red slippers. 'Going to a wake, I take it, dear?'

She classed all these details and my affairs generally as 'the doings of the Caravan.' Girlhood like this was a shock of welcome surprise to her.

She was interested in my music, acting quite rapt as I played my simple little pieces to her, all the way up to Mendelssohn and Beethoven; questioned me about the books I read, my parties and the partners I liked best. I took my favorites over now and then to stroll beneath her window, where she examined them through a swiftly drawn blind, reserving her decisions until I saw her next. At other times my young friends went with me into the closed double parlors to sing for her.

The walls were hung with heavily gold-framed engravings: 'The Forester's Family,' 'The Stag at Bay,' 'Arctic Night,' and other chastely cold subjects. The piano was an old-fashioned square in an elaborately carved mahogany case, and the carpet a fabulous Brussels, woven in a pattern. It had in the centre a great basket of flowers, from which roses were spilling all over the floor to a border of more flowers at the edge. It enjoyed a reputation of its own; and the day of my grandmother's funeral two old ladies came an hour ahead of the service 'to get a last look at the carpet before the mourners broke up the pattern.'

The wallpaper was white with large figures. The white marble mantels and the marble-topped tables added a chill even on hot midsummer afternoons.

One of those musical lads who oftenest sang there, a clergyman *emeritus* now, said to me recently: 'Singing in that old parlor—"In days of old, when Knights were bold"—to Miss Emily, awed me so that to this day I remember how I used to tiptoe all the way across the lawn to the other house afterward.'

Undoubtedly it was the son of her girlhood friend, Abbie Wood (Mrs. Daniel Bliss, of Beirut), who gave Aunt Emily her most constant musical delight.

Fred Bliss was a musician of rare natural gifts, playing Beethoven's sonatas, Schubert's songs, Schumann and Chopin, or bits of oratorio and opera that flitted through his head and fingers by the hour. I well remember how the 'Moonlight Sonata' sounded through the silence of the old house, or the 'Erl King,' which was always twice spectral in effect as he played it to his transported listener. From the time he came to Amherst to fit for college until his graduation in 1880, their friendship of music was unbroken, and as long as she lived he never returned to Amherst without playing for her.

Her friend, Mrs. Dole, well remembered still as an accomplished pianist of wide study, and taste respectfully alluded to as 'classical,' who often played in public for charitable objects under social wings, always enjoyed playing for Aunt Emily when the coast was clear of callers and the freedom of the house their own.

But of all her visitors, perhaps the 'excitingest' memory is that of a span of horses being walked up and down before the house while Helen Hunt went inside to see Aunt Emily. Many times the driver turned them around at the same tree, walked them as far as our own front gate, and turned them again, while we outside gave ourselves up to wonder as to what those two in the library were saying to each other. At last, after an hour or more, a figure appeared, ran down the terrace steps, sprang into the waiting carriage, and, with the *diminuendo* of horses' feet, life fell back to its old level.

We looked forward to Judge Lord, too, her father's friend, who continued his habit of coming every summer with his two nieces for a brief visit, giving us young folk trips to Mount Holyoke or Northampton in an open hack—thrilling in contrast to our country ways of driving—while Aunt Emily and he enjoyed their own adventures in conversation at home.

Except to the narrowing few of her chosen friends, inevitably Aunt Emily became something of a fable. Like the Shepherdess on Keats's 'Grecian Urn,' the more she eluded, the more she was pursued. If 'Miss Emily' could live without her fellow townsmen, they would not live without her.

It became something of a boast to have seen her. In spite of herself she seemed fated to be conspicuous in her very avoidance of notice. And with each passing year it grew more usual for even our own guests whom she loved, to come back, reporting a pleasant call at the Mansion—adding, rather crestfallen, 'But I did not see Emily.'

It puzzled women who wore sensible stuff dresses why Emily wore white the year around. Various fantastic tales were circulated about her. Sometimes such stories made us laugh; more often they made us hate the stupidity that invented them. She puzzled those people she was not just like, simply because she was not like everybody else of that day and place. 'Self-expression' was not in vogue in her day. It was hard to put up with in a country village. Why should she wear white? What good reason was there for her not doing exactly what everybody else did? What was she making a mystery about? And the only person who never thought of it as a mystery was Emily herself, as she moved about her father's house and garden. They could no more approach her than they could make the moon come down and sit on their parlor sofas!

Already the curious had begun to attempt to press in. Mere acquaintances, strangers even, baffled in their attempts to see Aunt Emily, sent her flowers, fruit, and other little offerings in the hope of an acknowledgment by one of her cryptic notes which could be later shown and boasted of. Being a gentlewoman, she often made whatever responses she did to avoid appearance of discourtesy, rather than from interest in the sender, of whose real motive she was, of course, totally unaware. And with the years, the necessity has almost arisen, as with Talleyrand, 'to defend her from having herself invented complications with which she is charged.'

Some of the tales told lacked all taste or personality, and my father shrank from them. He could never reconcile himself to her way of living that brought such ridiculous conjecture down upon her. He would have wished her happy and natural—although even in the same breath he could never wish her any different!

Of course she was a romantic figure.

Cornelia Mather (Mrs. Evans Kellogg) recalls that, as a child living with her aunt just across the street, she used to watch for a light behind 'Miss Emily's' window-shade at night and tell herself, with a shiver of excitement, 'I have seen Miss Emily's shadow!'

Even now a returning native of the village will say: 'When I was a boy at Amherst, I drove a grocer's cart, and once Miss Emily gave me a piece of cake. I never forgot it.'

Or some white-haired woman adds her memory of going as a little girl on an errand to the Mansion when 'Miss Emily' patted her red cheek and asked her what Baldwin apple she had rubbed it from.

In pleasant weather both aunts used to sit on the retired little side piazza, where we joined them singly or in twos and threes, grouping ourselves in chairs or on the steps at their feet, according to age and number. The giant *Daphne odora,* moved out from the conservatory, stood at one end with the cape jasmine. Two tall oleanders were blossoming in their green tubs, and a pomegranate whose flowering was an event to us all. The flagged path to the garden began here, leading down through the grass to a meandering mass of bloom. It was against Aunt Lavinia's will that anything there was ever uprooted or pruned. She adored profusion. The roses clapped their hands high over two old-fashioned arbors; the honeysuckle lured the humming-birds all day; nasturtiums pranked like unruly schoolboys; self-sown flowers of humbler origin elbowed and crowded their more aristocratic neighbors. There were carpets of lily-of-the-valley and pansies, platoons of sweet peas, hyacinths enough in May to give all the bees of a summer dyspepsia. There were ribbons of peony hedges, and rifts of daffodil in season, marigolds to distraction—a butterfly Utopia.

On these occasions it was Aunt Emily's way to listen more than she talked. She would sit motionless until impelled to hurl in some terse conclusion, or send up a verbal rocket, or toss a flower on the tranquil flow of conversation, as it chanced. Her more serious talk was oftenest reserved for quiet meetings with us one at a time. Detail was anathema to her, 'the mean terms' of life and thought were not for her.

She loved to fence in words with an able adversary. Circumlocution she despised. Her conclusions hit the mark and suggested only an arrow in directness, cutting the hesitancies of the less rapid thinker. She arrived at the heart of the matter with a velocity which made the ordinary processes of thought seem sluggish. She loved a metaphor, a paradox, a riddle; and she was both shy and enormously self-confident. Her imagination knew no hindrance, and the mystic in her gained immeasurably from her power to project herself into an abstraction, beyond the hindering visible limitations surrounding her.

Her sympathy with each one of us was inexhaustible. My father went to her, just as we all did, for response to many moods. If we were dull or disappointed, perplexed, or so happy we had to talk about it, Aunt Emily's wit, keen penetration, and eagerness were ours. As consoler she went all lengths, as when she wrote her sister Lavinia on the loss of a cat, that she will try to take

Pussy's place—and again begs her not to work and get tired, reminding her assuringly, 'I can sweep in the fall.'

My own especial liking was to slip over and sit by the table as the aunts were finishing their supper together—the frosted loaf cake about to be cut, the evening leisureliness upon them. We touched on many vital things then. The poignancy of Aunt Emily's voice as she exclaimed, 'You have been with Maggie and Philip in the Red Deeps, Matty!' made the one sentence an unforgettable appreciation of the 'Mill on the Floss.'[13] She had a way of alluding to and talking about the characters in books familiar to us both, as if they were people living right about us—the three Brontë girls were nearer to her than most such.

> Oh, what an afternoon for Heaven,
> When Brontë entered there!

she once wrote, reversing the accepted terms to suit her own conviction. But of all her adopted spiritual kin she identified herself closest with the Brownings. Robert Browning was in her eyes all a brave man and a poet might be to a frail, shy poet-woman like Elizabeth Barrett—or herself. In their fulfilled life she saw all that her own might have been—had her own romance been possible. His name stood to her as an image. She could

---

13 It is more than probable that her interest in the *Imitation* (Thomas à Kempis) was aroused by its influence over Maggie Tulliver. In the English edition given her by my mother, in which she had written Aunt Emily's name, she fifty years later wrote my own.

repeat it without speaking the one for which it stood in her own heart.

Was this, perhaps, in her mind when she would ask me, as an equal in age and understanding, her poignant question, 'Can you make life go about as you want it to these days, dear?' or her sweet 'What has grieved you, dear?' if I looked what she called 'solemn.'

Later she would come out and flit about the grounds with me—to the grape trellises to see if the green clusters were showing purple yet, on past the pear trees loaded with golden fruit, and my grandmother's row of fig trees which had been given to Aunt Emily and were her peculiar care, on even as far as the garden, if the evening was dry enough or a young moon enticed.[14] These were the very grapes and pears she would be sending later to her friends. No one loved to share as she did. Fresh-laid eggs, young chickens roasted by Maggie, the cake or winejelly of her own making—all went the same path with a nosegay on top to bless them—Aunt Emily's own grace. None of our guests failed to receive some greeting from her a cape jasmine from her own conservatory being the crowning attention. With one brought to my Aunt Mattie[15] on a visit to us she admits: 'I bring my first jasmine, minute and alone, but to me incomparably precious.'

In thinking back over the past now, nothing is more striking than the actual glamour Aunt Emily seems to

---

14 After her father's death she never went outside the hedge.
15 My mother's sister.

have cast over us—all the way from childhood on. She never had to say 'don't' to us. She never had to beg us to stop—to do this or that. When we were with her, our one wish was to speak softly and move deftly lest we wake up outside our happy moment.

As a child no sleigh-ride behind a horse girt with jangling bells counted with me if Aunt Emily would look out of her window as I coasted by on my green sled. As we grew older, the same sort of spell seems to have been over us all. Even my father would never go nearer her sacred centers than she indicated. Lovely as she was to us all, we stood in awe of an indefinable quality in her. I have seen her face stern, as if in judgment of her own soul or fate. She looked like my grandfather then—trying the Providence above her, perhaps, before her own tribunal. Hers was a rigor of personality quite consistent with complete affection for each one of the home circle, and this became increasingly apparent. Not that we were overshadowed; we were only the quicker to protect her from any clumsy or unwelcome intrusion from any direction. We never asked her questions about herself. We never tried to pry into the secret of her life or its power over us. Instinctively we wanted everything to be as she wanted it, her 'polar privacy' preserved.

Plato makes Socrates say, 'Everything is strange until the soul has found it to be familiar,' and it must be kept in mind that there was no time when Aunt Emily was not 'familiar' to us. We did not have to come upon her in middle life. She was in the midst of our life from the beginning of anything. We grew up with her, toward her—never to her, of course. She was part of childhood, youth, and our premonitions of manhood and woman-hood. We had no previous conception of her to harmo-nize with reality.

We had not conceived her in a mould into which for consistency's sake she must be run. We did not merely learn her from her poems and letters, but knew her as part of our every day. The little notes she sent to our mother and ourselves went hand in hand with Mother Goose. A beloved matter-of-course to us, we never rea-soned about her any more than how the tallest pine got where it was on the old driveway.

The death of my brother Gilbert in the autumn of 1883 kept me from school at Farmington that year, as none of us could bear the thought of further partings, and in the months that followed I found a new and different comfort with Aunt Emily.

Sometimes Aunt Lavinia would go sleigh-riding in my place with my brother Ned or my father of a win-ter's afternoon, and I would slip over by the narrow path walled in by snowdrifts to stay with Aunt Emily. She would perhaps be by the dining-room fire, or better still up in her own room, forever associated for me with the odor of hyacinths, for the way of a bulb in the sunshine had an uncanny fascination for her, their little pots crowding all four window-sills to bring a reluctant spring upon the air. From the first prick of the green above the earth she detected every minute sign of growth.

There I would find her reading or writing, while the slow glow of the open Franklin stove added another deceptive hint of spring warmth. And although I was but seventeen then, we talked of serious or imaginative things—situations in books or wondered about the future, gravely comparing our absurdly unequal conclusions—without a sign on her part of the crudity of mine. It was all over in a flash, just as it had been when I was left with her a child of five. No matter what lie the clock told about an hour or an hour and a half, those returning sleighbells jangling in brought me back from 'that little time upon enchanted ground.'

Once in that happy place I repeated to Aunt Emily what a neighbor had said—that time must pass very slowly to her, who never went anywhere—and she flashed back Browning's line:

Time, why, Time was all I wanted!

Another exciting line of his, quoted by her in face of domestic complications, with her pet gesture of bravado, was:

Who knows but the world may end tonight?

—as if for her part she wished it would—dared it to— would like to see it do it!

She was always sweetly welcoming, though any interruption must have cut in on that time she so wanted; for Aunt Emily was busy, always busy. When she read, she was next busiest to when she wrote. Downstairs with the family it was oftenest a Boston paper or the *Springfield Republican* she glanced over until the rest were happily employed, when she would sit straight up under the big readinglamp on the table and be lost to them in the book before her.

It must be recalled that her formative years belonged to a period of extreme romanticism, typified by Jean Paul Richter, and influenced to an incredible degree by his 'Life,' and later his 'Titan,' which were eagerly read and marked by them all, as the old copies attest.

Also, it was at that time that the New England Transcendentalists were developing their revolt against the commonplace in employment and society. Emerson was held to be sadly advanced by the elders, and a prophet of the new freedom by their sons and daughters. The experiments of Brook Farm and Thoreau's hut were infections Aunt Emily could not have escaped. There was much talk of following one's own star wherever it led, howbeit Puritan blood held them back when it came to setting forth. The expression and effect of all this must have been in her mind, though it could hardly be held in the least responsible for her refusal to compromise with her own jealous genius.

I could not have told when I first divined her by a higher sense than mere growing-up afforded me.

We had always known of her renunciation of the man she loved long before we were born. It was part of our consciousness of Aunt Emily. As a little girl the voices of concern overheard when my mother and her sister Mattie were speaking together of the sacrifice of her young romance echoed in my ears. It was perfectly understood in the family, but not talked about outside. It had all happened years before we children were born, though it seemed still so poignant to our elders. We accepted Aunt Emily just as we found her, just as she was, as we had any other phenomenon of Nature. First in her white dress she was to us a fairy to overcome whatever had 'grieved' us, then increasingly as a friend more rare than any other we knew.

I cannot tell when I first became aware that she had *elected* her own way of life. To us she had always been as fixed in her orbit as any other star. We had been born into her life. It never seemed to us that it should have been any other than it was.

In regard to his sister, my father was a victim of the prevalent scourge of dread of the New England village gossip concerning all unmarried women of that narrow time. He had what would seem to modern eyes a morbid horror of his sister Emily being thought to have been 'disappointed' in love. He never liked and would not even hear those of her poems sent over to my mother that were sad or suggested anything of that kind. His sister Lavinia shrank from this idea to an even greater degree. Both were New-Englanders of the old extreme type, suffering under conviction of a tradition now long gone—and almost forgotten.

It must be reiterated that they were all three of an era most exaggeratedly mid-Victorian. In addition to the proprieties and reticences which may now seem absurd, they grew up in the overshadowing atmosphere of a Puritan missionary college. Of the three, Aunt Emily herself would have been the most extreme in her aversion for having her romance a subject of public remark. It would have filled her with horror to have realized the idle curiosity about her and her private affairs, and her will, though unexpressed, emphasized their instinctive reserve. Her uncompromising conviction, that her life was sacred and of no legitimate concern to the public, constrained them; for with her gentleness, sensitiveness, and the shyness so popularly associated with her, went a tacit and coercive will and an unconscious power of personality that imposed its own terms. The attitude of her brother and sister was consequent upon their obligation as they saw it. What they did not foresee was that, with the publishing of the poems, in the whirligig of time posthumous fame was to deliver their sister Emily over to posterity, refusing her 'the right to perish' that she considered 'might be thought an undisputed right.'

> The right to perish might be thought
> An undisputed right.
> Attempt it, and the Universe upon the opposite

Will concentrate its officers—
You cannot even die,
But Nature and Mankind must pause
To pay you scrutiny.[16]

It was impressed on my brother and myself as early as I can remember, by both our parents, that Aunt Emily was not to be a subject of discussion with outsiders. The relatives and close friends of the family knew the situation perfectly, but of course my brother and I were often 'pumped' and subjected to close questioning by curious acquaintances—or even strangers. After one experience of this kind, when I had left my play and come home, not knowing what else to do, I asked my father what I should say when people like that plied me with questions about Aunt Emily, and he replied tersely: 'Tell them you don't know. Don't say a word more,' adding, 'But always remember, little girl, it is not in the highest taste to make remarks about things people don't talk about themselves and don't care to have talked about.' Nothing, perhaps, could so well indicate his feeling about it all—an instinct that has so often been referred to as 'the Dickinson reserve.'

I did not forget it. I drew my own conclusions and acted upon them. I argued there was something solemn about it all, something quite beyond me. It

---

16 *Poems of Emily Dickinson*, Centenary Edition, Little, Brown and Company, p. 224.

became a point of family loyalty to do exactly as I had
been told by my parents.[17]

---

17 Emily Dickinson never wished her romance probed. During her
lifetime she removed it from discussion. Inevitably, however, after the
publication of selections from her love poems in the nineties—given
to the world by her sister Lavinia—a supreme factor in my aunt's
development became self-evident. It became imperative to correct any
false impression. That whatever detail may inevitably have been more
or less blurred in the long passage of time, the inward drama of nearly
eighty years ago, and the unmitigated reaction produced upon her
whom it affected, no sincere reader can ignore, has been repeatedly
stressed by her public. Under the circumstances it seemed but due
the dead to indicate the befitting dignity of the true inspiration of
the love poems. The testimony of her closest contemporaries leaves
no doubt that during her visit to Philadelphia, following her stay in
Washington, my aunt met the man who was henceforth to stand to
her for the Power and the Glory, and with whom, in the phrase of the
day, she 'fell in love.' These contemporaries were agreed that any further development of what was stated to be their mutual recognition of
each other was impossible, owing to the fact that he was already married. According to them, the definite renunciation followed a brief
interview in her father's house, and left a permanent effect upon my
aunt's life and vision.

This was well known in the family, as well as by the relatives and closest friends. It was told me specifically by my father (Emily Dickinson's
only brother), by my Aunt Lavinia (her only sister), by my Aunt Mattie
Gilbert, who lived in Amherst at the time it occurred (Emily Dickinson's
close friendship with Mattie Gilbert is shown in her letters included in
this volume), and by my mother, also living in Amherst then with her
sister Harriette, being publicly engaged to my father and already called
'Sister Sue' in the letters of my Aunt Emily Dickinson, whose confidante
she was from girlhood to the day of Emily Dickinson's death.

It must never be lost sight of that the accepted social code of the
eighteen-fifties in New England had no hint of the code of today. The
painful scrupulousness and extreme sensitiveness of those old New
England families can only be intelligible to those who have known them
or belonged to them—scarcely even by such today. Moreover, no member of Emily Dickinson's family then living imagined the exact private
details of a most private life could ever be of the slightest legitimate im-
portance the outside world. They seem to have sharply distinguished to
their own satisfaction between the Poet in the abstract and their sister
as an individual, whose preferences it was their right to preserve intact.
And under this naive hallucination, as it evidently appears to modern
eyes they seem to have proceeded. Aunt Lavinia was a New-Englander
of New-Englanders. To her it was a sacrilege for any outsider to suppose

her idolized sister could have had a 'disappointment' in love. To the curious she denied it fiercely. Nevertheless, as series after series of the poems appeared, skeptical critics and readers declared the love poems could only have been written from personal experience. As one reviewer stated: 'There are poems here printed in respect to love that never could have been written without experience; the deepest feeling must have inspired them, and no one can read them without the conviction that Emily Dickinson knew what she was talking about.' Aunt Lavinia was aghast lest any hint of scandal, from her point of view, touch her sister. It was after the death of her nephew Edward (Ned) that she committed without reserve the trust of her sister Emily's life to her niece, who was to be her sole survivor and heir.

During the year of Aunt Emily's centenary, such baseless romances of eighty years ago were ignorantly accredited her by those more zealous than informed that letters from old family friends and relatives began to flow in, impatient for their repudiation. For example, the wife of one of Amherst College's oldest and most respected Trustees, who had known the Dickinson family intimately since girlhood, and who treasures notes from both Aunt Emily and Aunt Lavinia, wrote indignantly: 'After all these years it seems strange to have these love affairs trumped up. I remember your mother saying to me—just after Miss Lavinia's death that Emily had "met her fate" when she went South on a visit. That the love had been instant, strong, mutual—that she would go no further, tor it would mean sorrow to another woman—his wife. This is the story I've had in my mind all these years.'

The wife of a first cousin of Aunt Emily wrote: 'It was well understood by the family that Emily went on a trip to Washington to visit father, and on the way home stopped off for a visit in Philadelphia, where she met her fate, a young clergyman, who unfortunately was already married. Other stories about Emily's love affair have no foundation in fact. Mother also mentioned the fact of her habitual wearing of white which the family said was a sort of memorial to the man she love, whom she renounced. There is nothing more to be said, as this is the whole story.'

A great-granddaughter of Samuel Fowler Dickinson wrote: 'There was never any mystery about it in the family. It was well known who the man was. He was the clergyman of Philadelphia whom she met on her way back home. My father, who was her first cousin, my grandmother, who was the wife of Samuel Fowler Dickinson, Jr., and my Aunt Katherine Sweetser (Emily's father's sister) all knew it, and spoke of it openly.'

The writers of the above letters are known to the publishers. Their names are here withheld solely to prevent their annoyance through attempts at correspondence by strangers.

In spite of the impression deliberately created, by those nearest her in her own generation, that death had prematurely ended even 'the

In that loving silence my brother Ned and I allied ourselves to protect what we in our young ardor imagined to be Aunt Emily's 'feelings,' until, as I sat talking with her of many things, during the last few years she lived, I used to wonder if she knew I knew—as one in dreams wonders if the dead who stand before one so naturally, know that they are dead, with horror only lest a clumsy move lead them to suspect the truth. Just so I dreaded Aunt Emily's ever conceiving me as having transgressed her sacred places, sure that, as she had said of another, 'encroachment would have slain' her.

With the temerity of youth I often tried to draw her further from home, taking her hand and chatting as we strolled. But at the tall pine on the driveway she would stop, leaving me with the same gentle promise, 'Another night, dear.' The external life had definitely receded before the one of her choice.

Eventually it became a constant influence in the life of each one of us to know she was always there in her own place—a fixed entity. The fret of temporal servitudes did not exist for her. There was an exquisite self-containment about her from her very relinquishment of

---

right of surmising' further, Emily Dickinson's remaining relatives and the proved family friends were and are firmly united in this belief. Of unidentified tellers of tales, of whose *bonafides* I am uninformed, I can affirm nothing.

By those who reverence as well as admire Emily Dickinson, it may well be held that Louis Untermeyer was clairvoyant when he said: 'Emily tells the whole story of her love, her first rebellious desire, her inner negation, her resignation, her waiting for reunion in Eternity. There is nothing more to add except unimportant names and irrelevant street numbers.' (From 'Colossal Substance,' a review of *Further Poems of Emily Dickinson* in the *Saturday Review of Literature*, March 16, 1929.)

all part in outward event. Undistracted by conflicting or too numerous examples of beings, she could fully absorb herself in her abstractions, and a certain expression of detachment isolated her. Observing it, no one transgressed. The nature and destiny of the whole human enterprise grew to be her real preoccupation. Perhaps we balanced her life—were the dead weight in the scale to ensure a certain poise.

My father sometimes said it was queer that Sue was never shocked by sacrilege in Emily—even when she startled him—and he explained it by her sixth sense for Emily's real meaning. For Emily was often considered sacrilegious by the orthodox of her day—long before the later publication of such poems as:

> Of course I prayed—
> And did God care?
> He cared as much
> As on the air
> A bird had stamped her foot
> And cried 'Give me!'[18]

But Susan knew that Emily, like others of her period, was involved in the conflict of old and new ideas in New England much to blame for our own non-conforming spirit. Like Emerson's mother, she was in fact 'holding on to the faith of past generations with both hands, yet all the time she doubted it.' She also had the same 'fatal

---

18 *Poems of Emily Dickinson*, Centenary Edition, Little, Brown and Company, p. 296.

gift of penetration, love of philosophy and impatience with words, doing their best to make a religious sceptic of her.' Yet even so, spurning all canting phrases, Emily remained a docile child of God and a rebellious heir of His kingdom. Susan realized that, although Emily took liberties with the Puritan vernacular and dogma when venting her baffled impatience with the Inscrutable, these impish flashes were no more to the underlying God-consciousness of the real Emily than the gargoyle on the roof is to the heart of the Cathedral within.

Whatever my mother's idea of Emily's ultimate recognition may have been, she never suggested her own estimates should be ours. Each one of us for ourselves made our own discovery of her at-homeness with disembodied thought. To come upon her suddenly, looking up into the tops of the trees, as if listening, not to the sounds of common day, not to her own thoughts, but to a mystic inclusion in some higher beauty known only to herself, forbade that we should fully interpret her. Nor was she lacking in a sort of spiritual arrogance—the right of one to whom much is revealed.

Indeed, her concentration on any object of her contemplation was so intense, it seemed to demobilize all her forces save those she projected upon that focus outside herself. Her mind seemed equally to go out to a thought or an inanimate thing brought to her close attention. She left her body behind at such times, just as, in contrast, when she cooked, she 'closed the valves of her attention' to the things preëminently of the spirit.

I never saw her angry except when someone had hurt or been false to one she loved. Then, let the betrayal be small or great, her loyalty brought fire to the brown eyes, a catch in her breath, and a stab in her terse, scathing words. Even so, the spirit of the consoler followed instantly. She was all tenderness, all eagerness to heal and fortify.

The early recollections we children had of Aunt Emily's lines, as she sent them to our mother, grew in understanding year by year. The real perception of her came much as the feeling of snow in the air to those New England born, by a conviction within, long before the first flake leaves the sky. Our immature pity for her self-imposed rigors, the narrow confines of her strait-ened life, deepened, became aware of her concern with dimensions beyond our conceiving. The perspective had changed. We were those hemmed in. Aunt Emily was free to her chosen horizon. However life might obstruct her feet, her spirit knew its way out. She had found and taken the one way her boat could sail, straight toward its sea. A mystic in that she grew so closely in contact with hidden forces, it was almost a psychic experience to get the manifestations she did. Yet her hold on the outward realities never weakened.

After she had lost both parents, Dr. Holland, 'Uncle Sam' Bowles, and almost all her fond, faraway chorus had gone into silence, she still had us of the 'beloved household.' And although she saw practically no one outside the family in those last few years, she did con-tinue to write her notes of occasion to her circle of friends and neighbors, not wishing them to feel she forgot or slighted whatever caused them joy or sorrow. It was the custom of country village life as it was lived in New England in the seventies and eighties. She was herself in these as in all she wrote.

Often these notes had a peculiar charm from their association. For example, this one to Margaret Tuckerman[19] on her first birthday—sent with red lilies from the conservatory:

> Let me commend Baby's attention to the only
> Commandment I ever kept—
>   'Consider the lilies.'
>
> E. DICKINSON

Still cherished in the recollection of Daniel Chester French[20] is the letter sent him after the unveiling of the Minute Man at Concord on the nineteenth of April, 1875:

> Dear Mr. French,
> We note with delight the recognition of a fame
> so eloquently won. All fame is dust, but a clay
> forever tinged with gold.
>   God keep you fundamental.
>
> E. DICKINSON

---

19 Now Mrs. Orton Clark.

20 The death of Mr. French has occurred since this was written.

The year I was at school at Farmington, except for my vacations, which were always met by her welcoming flowers or cakes, my brother Ned was the only one of our generation left to Aunt Emily. As he grew older, their tastes and the kinship of their ideas were always asserting themselves. They shared their discoveries in books, Ned carrying his wider adventures in newer authors to her and his flair for foreign politics and world affairs, of which she was a greedy listener. Through him she found her window to the outside world; through her he was finding his window to the Unseen—a reality to her.

Sometimes they were gay—the ludicrous and droll side of things uppermost. Or he would repeat to her some saying of Professor Garman to his psychology classes. But after our brother Gilbert's death, they were oftenest gravely speculative. Her spirit was reaching after him.

We both quoted her own lines to her many times without the slightest recognition on her part of where we had found them. With my mother she spoke simply enough of her verses, if they were alone. She never confided in her sister Lavinia as to the extent of her work. And though a large proportion of the poems found after Aunt Emily's death were perfectly familiar to 'Sister Sue,' to whom hundreds of them had been sent, Aunt Lavinia was unprepared for the discovery of the poems as afterward published, supposing her sister's countless letters and notes, often poems in themselves, sufficient to account for her habit of writing.

There were copies of poems sent her friends, variants and fragments found lying loosely in boxes and drawers; but inside her own bureau were the little packages tied with all sorts of cotton strings for hinges, with her most cherished correspondence—all marked to be burned at her death. She had seen it coming and had even made Maggie promise to carry out her wishes, as Maggie sobbed out to us, torn by her own conflicting loyalties. This was understood by Aunt Lavinia and my father and mother as no more than the final gesture of her unconquerable mortal shyness—something that had no longer any hold on the immortal Emily within her—and only the letters from others were destroyed.

Whatever her way of writing, upstairs in her own room, watching with her plants lest they freeze in zero midnights, or by the little table in the dining room, it was, as Mr. J. C. Squire has said, 'with the jerky and the elusive style we are much more familiar than anybody in England or America was in Emily Dickinson's time. But not with so much 'content.' There was never a trace of affectation in her when she was most moved, most sincere. It is probable, considering how widely she read and how much she respected art, that she might (had she lived) have remodeled her poems and tried to give them more of a conventional form. We may be glad she didn't. They are a direct message from mind and heart to mind and heart, and we can hear her voice in them.'[21]

---

21 J. C. Squire in a review of *Further Poems of Emily Dickinson* in the London *Observer*.

Nor was her reticence altogether singular. It has been pointed out that William Cullen Bryant, her poet neighbor of the Cummington Hills, evinced the same indifference to publication, putting his 'Thanatopsis' away in a drawer, where it lay for six years waiting to be discovered by his father.

Art—like spring—'came slowly up our way.'

My first meeting with Colonel Higginson was on the day of Aunt Emily's funeral.[22] Knowing, as I

---

22 I was present at the funeral of my grandfather, of my grandmother, of my Aunt Emily, and of my Aunt Lavinia. No member of the family ever lay after death in the parlor, as has been repeated by a recent writer. The stately front hall was invariably used, except for Aunt Emily, whose coffin was brought down from her room shortly before the service and placed in the library, where her family surrounded it. The old friend who dressed her for the grave wrote me the year of the 'centenary':

> Your mother came to me when Miss Emily died and said, 'When we come into the world we are wrapped in soft, white flannel, and I think it fitting that we leave it that way.' So I made a robe of the softest, finest flannel and personally put it on your Aunt Emily. I had only one fleeting vision of her while living, but in death her face had a serenity and sweetness which truly reflected the spirit gone before.
>
> 'Very sincerely your friend,
> 'EUNICE R. POWELL.

The assertion of a recent writer that the bearers at the funeral were college students is incorrect. Possibly the fact that at the funeral of my young brother Gilbert, several years earlier, the coffin was carried, with two exceptions, by college friends of my brother Ned might account for the confusion of some faulty memory. In the *Life and Letters (Life and Letters of Emily Dickinson*, Houghton Mifflin Company, pp. 101-02), I gave a literal account of Aunt Emily's funeral, stating that she was borne across the fields to her grave by laborers, all of whom a worked on her father's land. Mr. Ellery Strickland, the funeral director, a lifelong resident of Amherst, writes me of being called in after Aunt Emily's death and of being surprised to find her so young-looking, her reddish, bronze hair without a silver thread. 'How well I remember her passing to join the others,' he states, 'your mother and Mrs. Powell planning the robe . . . Then the cortège across the lawn, through the hedge, across the fields, a special bier borne by faithful workmen of her father's grounds, do now, that 'the New England coteries were united in the service of the conventional,' I see how it was typified in him. It was a sentimental age on both sides of the Atlantic, evidenced by the eleven hundred and thirty-six pages of the Brownings' love letters. Mrs. Sigourney and Elizabeth Barrett must have been far more to his faith. Amherst was farther from Boston and Cambridge then than now. Moreover, *nothing* could be more fatal to knowing Aunt Emily on her own terms than to take her literally when her mood was hyperbolic.[23]

Her friend Samuel Bowles rated this quality in her above all others, and called her 'his rascal.' Aunt Lavinia said that once, when he had driven from Springfield to see her, she refused to come down from some whim, and he ran part-way up the stairs calling, 'Emily, Emily, you rascal!—come down here!' And when she finally did, the call was more electric than ever.

It is this element of drollery in her, the elfin, mischievous strain, that is hardest for those who never knew her to reconcile with her solemn side. And in this mood the commonplace mind, however assiduous in pursuit,

---

Dennis Scanlon, Owen Courtney, Pat Ward, Steven Sullivan, Dennis Cashman, and Dan Moynihan.'

23 The claim made by a recent writer that since Emily wrote to Colonel Higginson, living at that time in Worcester, after his unsigned leading article, 'Letters to a Young Contributor,' in the *Atlantic Monthly* for April, 1862, she must have learned of his identity from George Gould, also in Worcester, may be dismissed in view of the fact that a review of the April *Atlantic*, with enthusiastic recommendations of the value of Colonel Higginson's advice to young writers, his name being given as the author of the article in question, appeared in the *Springfield Republican* (March 29, 1862), a paper which she read daily.

could never overtake her. 'Whimsy,' 'playing naïve' for sheer glee of her game— 'elfing it' we called the sport. At such times she was just Emily the 'rascal'—having fun with her audience, to the confusion of the matter of fact.

All three of them, sisters and brother alike, habitually burlesqued each other, satirized each other, made fun of each other's little foibles or pretensions. This form of domestic comedy was their way of making their own amusement as they went along in a world leaning toward solemnity. They saw through each other's little shams with clear eyes, and were too true to each other to fear or grudge the passing entertainment each afforded in turn.

Nor was their father left severely out of all this, Aunt Emily's attitude toward him being one of taking liberties, or mock awe, as her mood might be. Aunt Lavinia used to tell how once, when some message of his to the man about the frogs in the lower meadow had not been executed with becoming dispatch, their father took his hat and cane in high dudgeon, and walked out, remarking haughtily, 'I'll speak to the frogs myself about it!'—too vexed to notice his absurd slip of the tongue, and was met by Emily on his return with 'Did you find the frogs deferential, Father?'

Yet after his death she could never speak of him to us without tears. 'You must remember your grandfather. You must—you must *never* forget him as long as you live——' she would begin, breaking off, unable to control her quivering lips. And he has gone on astonishingly in my memory; walking stiffly, his mouth firmly set, yet with a smile not far off if occasion justified it, his eyes warmed by a curious kind of sparkle, his auburn coloring making him look young beside his white-haired neighbors; and always seeming somehow to stand between us all—at both houses—and any harm that could happen to us.

If Aunt Emily ever exclaimed with bated breath, 'This, then, is a book!'—how indisputably the rogue was uppermost, for her father's library, always under her hand, climbed from floor to ceiling, including not only complete sets of the more sedate British poets, but various editions of the work of Lord Byron, that elegant object of the lifted eyebrow of a hundred years ago. Books were the accompaniment of her days and nights from her youth up; and her three poems beginning, 'Unto my books how good to turn,' 'A precious mouldering pleasure 'tis to meet an antique book,' and 'There is no frigate like a book,' are among her most familiar and oft-quoted lines.

The little mental trapeze acts she performed for herself kept her spirits agile. When the family, leaving her alone while they went to church, contrived amusements to keep her from being lonely, had she not written when she was twenty, 'Lonely indeed!—they didn't look, and couldn't have seen if they had, who should bear me company . . . God is sitting right here—looking right into my very soul'—a dramatization of Omnipresence to take the breath of her contemporaries?

It cannot be too strongly urged that there is no accounting for Aunt Emily's countless contradictions and inconsistencies by 'the rule of three.' No one who knew her would attempt it. Had they been specially designed to defy classroom analysis and annoy the pedant—instead of being, as they were, the mere 'sport of spontaneity'—their effect could not have been better calculated.

I remember telling her how, when a child, I once had been sent up to the guest-room to sit quietly by myself as a punishment—until I regretted some trifling dereliction; but I had enjoyed the pretty room so much I had refused to come out when the ban was lifted, and how her eyes sparkled as she confided to me, joyously, 'Matty, child, no one could ever punish a Dickinson by shutting her up alone.' And in 1883, when I took her my Shakespeare birthday book for her signature, she highly approved the quotation opposite December 10: 'I hear, yet say not much, but think the more.' (*Henry VI,* Act 4, Sc. 1.)

Her love of being alone up in her room was associated with her feeling for a key, which signified freedom from interruption and the social prevention that beset her downstairs. She would stand looking down, one hand raised, thumb and forefinger closed on an imaginary key, and say, with a quick turn of her wrist, 'It's just a turn—and freedom, Matty!' She read her letters here, never opening one until she was alone—not even so much as a note from a neighbor. Her loneliness has been much deplored; but where and with whom would she not have been lonely? Her kind of loneliness was the gift whose riches she herself pronounced beyond the power of 'mortal numeral to divulge.' And what society of her contemporaries would have made up to her for the loss of that precious guest of her solitude she named 'Finite Infinity'?

The last time she ever came across the lawn to our house was in the night—long past midnight. My brother Ned was ill with an acute attack of rheumatism, affecting his heart. This was during the summer of 1883. We were all up and the house brightly lighted. The downstairs bedroom was full of the scent of the big sweetbriar rosebush just outside, and, as I went to close a window, there Aunt Emily stood.

'Is he better?—oh, is he better?' she whispered. Startled by the sight of her there alone at that hour, I only nodded assurance and hurried to the door, but before I could get to her, she was gone. I could not even see her disappear in the darkness.

A slow victim of Bright's disease during the last two years of her life, she was at first quite like herself when we saw her, though as it went on she was often too frail to bear the effort of long talking. She only admitted herself 'ill since November' of that final year, and more than ever one got the impression of her own rapt absorption in something beyond us all—something of a consequence beyond the visible to which she was related.

When she was able to see us at all, I never saw her look or act ill. Always she preserved that same impression of youth. Her deep Titian hair never got a grey thread. Her white skin never showed a blemish, its lack of color unnoticeable because habitual. There was no less drama in the movement of her dainty hands. Age never benumbed her.

And during this last interval her messages to my mother still came over, startling as ever but increasingly poignant—

Be Sue while I am Emily. Be next, what you have ever been, Infinity.

And this:

The tie between us is very fine, but a hair never dissolves.

Lovingly,

EMILY

Her impatience with detail and what she termed 'mere fact' grew upon her, in her search for truth. It was the principle beyond the truth that she was after, the source of light beyond the pine trees; and not only the principle, but its ultimate significance. As death took from her one after another of those she had most loved, she apparently became more preoccupied with Eternity, not as an abstraction, but a further phase of life and love.

Whatever the despair of those days that had once 'unrolled as huge as yesterdays in pairs,' Emily had found their answer and was setting it down. In ways 'she knew not that she knew,' 'with sinews from within,' the Faith of her Fathers was with her yet. How ignorantly or willfully they err who doubt her loneliness was inherent, or urge that any manner of outside sympathy could have fully sufficed or any human relations sustained her! How could she escape the God-haunted ancestry from which she had sprung?

It was on a May morning when my father, hastily summoned to her, came back for my mother, telling us that Aunt Emily had fainted and fallen, losing consciousness suddenly. This time it was the end.

The day seemed strangely still as we went back and forth, not seeing the violets in the grass or hearing the birds, just waiting, staying near, longing for her to know that we were there.

From the coma into which she sank, she never waked; and when we knew she would not, we went about saying to each other—as she had said of Charlotte Brontë—'Oh, what an afternoon for Heaven!'

Nothing could be more false than any picture of Emily Dickinson suppressed or constrained to any course against her will. It was the object of her sister Lavinia's later life to preserve for her the solitude she then sought, which was a part of her and made her what she was. As a girl in Amherst, she had more opportunities than most of her companions. The hospitality of her father's house is still spoken of. She made frequent visits upon her relatives in Boston; she made a visit with the family in Washington where her father was in Congress, and is recorded by contemporaries as being remembered by those she met for her wit. Her own home was pervaded, animated, dominated by her; and her brother's home was hers when she would—with all it had to offer in devotion and companionship.

Their spontaneous affection for their home is repeated in the letters of both Aunt Emily and her brother Austin. Every door of her father's house flung wide signified to her a welcome home—not a setting forth.

Aunt Emily chose to withdraw from the world, not all at once, not definitely at first, but gradually, irresistibly—as her own work and premonition drew her. And if here she 'wrought with sad sincerity' at times, had she set out into the world of eighty years ago, what imaginable compensation could any career then open to her have offered the *real* Emily Dickinson? Her essential rebellion was against Life defrauded of the truth about Death. It was her Tyrant need-to-know that shut her in and left her knocking— 'knocking everywhere.'

It is the final paradox of a supreme Paradoxer that Emily Dickinson, who fled all publics, all renowns, should only have run the faster toward her own. Yet it is in entire accord with her own prophecy—

Eternity will be
Velocity or pause
Precisely as the candidate
Preliminary was.

II
A HEDGE AWAY
1856-62

Emily's only brother, Austin, was married on July 1, 1856, and from that time she was part of every incident in his household. Her first little note to his wife, with which 'The Single Hound' is prefaced, expressed her feeling perfectly:

> One sister have I in our house
> And one a hedge away—
> There's only one recorded
> But both belong to me.

In the years following that crucial visit to Washington and Philadelphia, her life moved on without external change, except that she imperceptibly but increasingly withdrew from outside festivities and public appearances and became less accessible to all save her chosen few. But her brother's marriage brought a thrilling new element into her life, and she continued to flit across the intervening lawns behind the bulwark of high hemlock hedges long after all other visits had definitely ceased. The narrow path 'just wide enough for two who love' ran luringly between, whether her light flashed across the snow to them under a polar moon, while she sat up to watch over her flowers and keep them from freezing, or past the rosebushes of a midsummer, where the moths were at their amorous trafficking.

Emily's own conservatory was like fairyland at all seasons, especially in comparison with the dreary white winter cold outside. It opened from the dining-room, a tiny glass room, with white shelves running around it on which were grouped the loveliest ferns, rich purple heliotrope, the yellow jasmine, and one giant *Daphne odora* with its orange-bloom scent astray from the Riviera, and two majestic cape jasmines, exotics kin to her alien soul. She tolerated none of the usual variety of mongrel houseplants. A rare scarlet lily, a resurrection calla, perhaps—and here it was always summer with the oxalis dripping from hanging baskets like humble incense upon the heads of the household and its frequenters.

When her brother's first son was born, named for his grandfather, her flying little greeting to him—delivered at her sister's pillow—was:

Is it true, dear Sue?
Are there Two?

I shouldn't like to come
For fear of joggling Him!
If you could shut him up
In a coffee cup,
Or tie Him to a pin
Till I got in,
Or make Him fast
To Pussy's fist,
Hist! Whist!
I'd come!

EMILY

Later, with her little niece, and the golden-haired arch-darling of both houses—the transitory child, Gilbert, who only came and flashed a mere eight years and went on—Emily was just another child like them, only endowed with subtle powers of the high gods to produce unexpected rewards and avert disastrous consequences. No treat could be offered any one of the three like that of being left in her care while the grown-up family wandered. As they grew older, she made companions of them, talked to them as equals, trusted them with her choicest interests. To them her increasing solitude never seemed strange; love gave them understanding. Had she worn wings instead of her simple white frocks, they would have taken it quite for granted.

Until she was obliged to go to Boston for treatment of her eyes in 1864 and again in 1865 the events in

Emily's life were counted as with Shakespeare's clock—'by heart-throbs, not by hours.'

As her brother's family grew up, she accepted them one by one, an individual relation existing between each of the three and her fairy self. When her little niece began her first attempts to write her own fancies in verse, Emily's response came quickly back, 'I was surprised, but why? Is she not of the lineage of the spirit?' She always alluded to the youngest son, Gilbert, as 'Thy Son, our Nephew.' As she put the world further from her their triple alliance increased in intimacy. She hailed them as treading where she dared not venture, bade them come back and tell her their adventures, was curious about their thoughts and tiny events which gave her escape from her own limited environment, which she loved, yet endured.

Though she dwelt only 'a hedge away' from their home, she had the habit of sending her constant thought to them in her tiny notes as other people would have spoken them. The gambol of her mind on paper was her pastime. Sometimes her mood was one of sheer extravaganza—like this:

Friday Noon

Dear Friend

I regret to inform you that at three o'clock yesterday my mind came to a stand, and has since then been stationary. Ere this intelligence reaches you I shall probably be a snail. By this untoward Providence a mental and moral being has been swept ruthlessly from her sphere. But we should not repine—'God moves in a mysterious way his wonders to perform,' and if it be his will that I become a bear and bite my fellow men, it will be for the highest good of this fallen and famishing world. If the gentleman in the air will please stop throwing snowballs, I may meet you again. Otherwise it is uncertain. My parents are pretty well. General Wolf is here. We are looking for Major Pitcairn in the afternoon stage. We were much afflicted yesterday by the supposed removal of our cat from time to eternity. She returned however last evening, having been detained by the storm beyond her expectations.

We need some paths up our way, shan't you be out with the team?

Yours till death

ISAIAH

The stately old barn was an equine palatial structure, sheltering horses, cows, pigs, hens, and pigeons, with wings for musty carriage houses, and leaning ramparts of loft where swallows darted and doves eternally gurgled. The animal traffic out there had a charm for Emily, and her wit often pranked with its daily round. Wanting her nephew once to the rescue she sends this:

Ned

Dennis was happy tonight and it made him graceful. I saw him waltzing with the cow and suspected his status. You told me he had not tasted liquor since his wife's decease—then she must have been alive at six this evening. I fear for the rectitude of the barn. Love for the Police.

EMILY

Her Christmas offering of iced plum cake and candy was once sent in the afternoon and with it this apology:

Sister

Please excuse Santa Claus for calling so early, but gentlemen 1882 years old are a little fearful of the evening air.

And in the early days of the very last spring of her life, to Gib the characteristic lines:

> Not at home to callers
> Says the naked tree —
> Jacket due in April.
> Wishing you good day.

There are still endless little notes sent in every possible phase of her mood. Comments on books she read, cries of the heart, dashes of wit; and when her habit of writing became confirmed, poems for suggestion, or criticism. From the time Emily had taken the dare of thirty, that 'frightful age' spoken of with bated breath in their teens by her sister Lavinia, the notes were often those same poems afterward published, sent either as an expression of an emotion she wished to share, or with a request for criticism.

In an article upon her unpublished letters to her brother's family, which appeared in the *Atlantic Monthly*, it has been told of her that these notes

> contained numberless phrases of universal truth, written though they were by this shy recluse in her retired New England home, intrenched by lilacs and guarded by bumble bees . . . She had her finger on the pulse of events and noted phenomena unerringly, with her own comment. Whenever stirred, by whatever cause, she trapped her mood, then waited for her messenger, as vigilant as any spider . . . Emily Dickinson differed from all the women letter-writers of France and England in her scorn of detail, scarcely hitting the paper long enough to make her communication intelligible.

The following brief note is quoted from the same source:

> Opinion is a flitting thing
> But truth outlasts the sun,

If then we cannot own them both,
Possess the oldest one.

And this one:

When we have ceased to crave
The gift is given
For which we gave the earth
And mortgaged heaven,
But so declined in worth —
'Tis ignominy now to look upon.

Life had for her an infinite and increasing fascination. 'Are you sure we are making the most of it?'
she wrote on a slip of paper and sent over by hand just
because she was quick with the thrill of another day.
Again she sent the following:

Dear Sue —
A fresh morning of life and its impregnable
chances and the dew for you!

EMILY

Other quotations from the same articles show her
response to every appeal.

To the faithful absence is condensed presence.
To the others,—but there are no others.

So busy missing you I have not tasted Spring. Should there be other Aprils we will perhaps dine.

I must wait a few days before seeing you. You are too momentous,—but remember dear, it is idolatry, not indifference.

Her notes to the three children were their keen delight, and preserved by them beyond all their other treasures. No one but their Aunt Emily could have written, 'Emily knows a man who drives a coach like a thimble and turns the wheel all day with his heel. His name is Bumble Bee!' At the close of a letter to her older nephew away on a visit as a child, she writes:

Dear Ned-Bird —

It will be good to hear you again. Not a voice in the woods is so sweet as yours. The robbins have gone, all but a few infirm ones,—and the Cricket and I keep house for the frost. Good-night little brother. I would love to stay longer. Vinnie and Grandma and Maggie all give their love. Pussy her striped respects.

NED'S MOST LITTLE AUNT EMILY

When sending him a tiny pie:

Dear Ned:

You know that pie you stole? Well, this is that pie's brother. Mother told me when I was a boy, that I must turn over a new leaf. I call that the foliage admonition. Shall I commend it to you?

EMILY

On the birthday of her little niece she sends a knot of her choicest flowers and this word of greeting—

Dear Mattie—

I am glad it is your birthday. It is this little bouquet's birthday too. Its Father is a very old man by the name of Nature, whom you never saw. Be sure to live in vain, dear. I wish I had.

EMILY

The following chronicle came to Gilbert's mother after the rescue of a favorite cat by his Aunt Lavinia:

Memoirs of little boys that Live
'Weren't you chasing Pussy?' said Vinnie to Gilbert.

'No, she was chasing herself.'

'But wasn't she running pretty fast?'

'Well, some fast and some slow,' said the beguiling villain. Pussy's Nemesis quailed. Talk of hoary reprobates! Your urchin is more antique in wiles than the Egyptian sphinx. Have you noticed Granville's letter to Lowell? 'Her Majesty has contemplated you; and reserved her decision.'

It was, as Colonel Higginson once observed later on, a pretty rarefied atmosphere for children, but they regarded their Aunt Emily as a magical creature, and were brought up on her stabbing wit, her condensed forms and subtle epigram, and felt a lively contempt for people who said they could not understand her when their mother sometimes read out sentences or poems of hers to the curious who begged to hear something she had written. They felt she was always on their side, a nimble as well as a loving ally. She never dulled their sunshine with grown-up apprehensions for their good, or hindered their imagination, but rather flew before, like Aurora, straight out into the ether of the impossible, as dear to her as to them.

The following she sent to Ned after some reputed indiscretion reported of him by harder hearts:

> The cat that in the corner sits
> Her martial time forgot—
> The rat but a tradition now
> Of her desireless lot,
> Another class reminds me of—
> Who neither please nor play,
> But—'not to make a bit of noise'
> Adjure each little boy!

P.S. Grandma characteristically hopes Neddy will be a good boy. Obtuse ambition of Grandma's!

EMILY

On returning a photograph of a child in Greenaway costume:

That is the little girl I meant to be and wasn't; the very hat I meant to wear and didn't.

One verse she sent them that particularly hit their fancy was:

That butterfly in honoured dust
Assuredly will lie,
But none will pass his catacomb
So chastened as the fly.

One sent at Christmas with a beautifully iced cake was:

The Saviour must have been a docile
Gentleman
To come so far, so cold a night
For little fellow men.
The road to Bethlehem—
Since He and I were boys—
Has levelled—but for that 'twould be
A rugged billion miles.

To Ned after being severely stung by a hornet:

Dear Ned—
You know I never *did* like you in those 'yellow-jackets'!

EMILY

To Gilbert, a child in kindergarten then, she sent this, accompanied with a dead bee:

THE BUMBLE BEE'S RELIGION
For Gib to carry to his teacher from Emily
His little hearse-like figure
Unto itself a dirge,
To a delusive lilac
The vanity divulge
Of industry and morals
And every righteous thing,
For the divine perdition
Of Idleness and Spring.

'All liars shall have their part.' Jonathan Edwards.
'And let him that is athirst come.' Jesus.

She furthered their childish love of mystery and innocent intrigue on every occasion, purloining for them any treat from the family supplies she could lay her fond hands upon.

Once with sweets smuggled over to them came these laconic instructions:

Omit to return box. Omit to know you received box.

BROOKS OF SHEFFIELD

At another like occasion:

The joys of theft are two; first theft; second supe-
riority to detection. How inspiring to the clan-
destine mind. 'We thank thee, Lord, that Thou
hast hid these things!'

She did a deal of brilliant trifling apropos of local
events. On the death of the wife of a doctor she disliked
she writes:

Deas Sue —
    I should think she would rather be the Bride
of the Lamb than that old pill box!

EMILY

With a cape jasmine sent to a guest of her niece as
yet unknown to her (Sara Colton Gillett) she writes:

M. will put this little flower in her friend's
hand. Should she ask who sent it, tell her—as
Desdemona did when they asked who slew
her—Nobody—Myself.

After the death of a strictly dull acquaintance with
no vital spark visible she writes:

Now I lay thee down to sleep,
I pray the Lord thy dust to keep,

If thou should *live* before thou wake,
I pray the Lord thy soul to make!

This scrap is Emily at her most audacious:

My Maker, let me be
Enamoured most of Thee—
But nearer this
I more should miss!

In a panic lest some cherished plan fall through she
sent this:

Boast not myself of to-morrow, for I 'knoweth
not' what a noon may bring forth.

This, too, is Emily to the core:

Cherish power dear; remember that it stands in
the Bible between the kingdom and the glory
because it is wilder than either.

The instances cited are characteristic of varying
moods. Her passion for brevity always deducted relentlessly. She refuses an invitation thus:

Thanks, Sue, but not to-night. Further nights.

EMILY

After some flashing pleasure given her she replies:

Don't do such things. Your Arabian Nights unfits the heart for its arithmetic.

Emily is sorry for Susan's day. To be singular under plural circumstances is a becoming heroism.

Susan knows she is a siren and at a word from her Emily would forfeit righteousness.

A spell cannot be tattered and mended like a coat.

No message is the utmost message, for what we tell is done.

To lose what we have never owned might seem an eccentric bereavement, but Presumption has its own affliction as well as claim.

The things of which we want the proof are those we know the best.

Where we owe but little we pay. Where we owe so much it defies money we are blandly insolvent.

Has *All* a codicil?

In a life that stopped guessing, you and I should not feel at home.

Tasting the honey and the sting should have ceased with Eden. Pang is the past of peace.

'To multiply the harbors does not reduce the sea,' defines her constancy.

'Emblem is immeasurable, that is why it is better than fulfillment, which can be drained'—reveals her elusive quality.

And how much she crowded into one sparse sentence when she said:

Danger is not at first, for then we are unconscious, but in the slower days.

Her letters sent when her family were really at a distance are never like those of any one else, and usually reflect the day and season more than any personal happenings. Across one runs this postscript:

Father's sister is dead, and Mother wears a black ribbon on her bonnet.

But usually they were more like this, one chosen at random:

Nothing is gone, dear, or no one that you know. The forests are at home, the mountains intimate at night and arrogant at noon. A lonesome fluency abroad, like suspended music.

Further on in the same letter:

Come home and see your weather; the hills are full of shawls. We have a new man whose name is Tim. Father calls him 'Timothy' and the barn sounds like the Bible.

Twilight touches Amherst with his yellow glove. Miss me sometimes, dear, not on most occasion, but in the Sometimes of the mind.

The small heart cannot break. The ecstasy of its penalty solaces the large.

Emerging from an abyss and reëntering it, that is Life, dear, is it not?

There were no so gay hours in Emily's life as those spent at her brother's home when there were guests of their own inner circle, who revelled in her companionship. For her own life never lacked its joy in comedy nor was her spirit quenched by its most subduing contact with the elemental tragedy that was constant to her thought. When Mrs. Anthon, of London, and Samuel Bowles, of the *Springfield Republican*, were there they played wild games of battledore and shuttlecock in the long winter evenings; Emily convulsing their onlookers by her superfluous antics added to their game. She improvised brilliantly upon the piano all sorts of dramatic performances of her own, one she called the Devil being particularly applauded.

It was on one of these winter nights of revel that they forgot the hour and suddenly, unwarned by the approaching beams of his lantern across the snow, became aware of her father's presence in their midst, to enquire the meaning of such prolonged hours. Emily is said to have drooped and disappeared before him like the dew, without a sound, but with a wicked glance or gesture to assert her unreconcilement to the proceedings.

Her sister Sue recognized her genius from the first, and hoarded every scrap Emily sent her from the time they were both girls of sixteen. Their love never faltered or waned. Emily pictures their first meeting and its changelessness:

> As much now as when love first began—on the step at the front door, under the evergreens.

One of her very last pencilled lines was this:

> With the exception of Shakespeare you have told me more knowledge than anyone living. To say that sincerely is strange praise.
>
> EMILY

Sometimes Emily addressed her as 'You from whom I never run away'; and again she exclaims:

> Susan! I would have come out of Eden to open the door for you if I had known you were there. You must knock with a trumpet as Gabriel does, whose hands are small as yours. I knew he knocked and went away—I did not dream you did!
>
> EMILY

And again:

To see you unfits for stabler meetings. I dare not
risk an intemperate moment before a banquet
of bran.

The decision to publish 'The Single Hound,' the
poem of their lifetime, was determined by a faded little
note of her early twenties:

Dear Sue—I like your praise because I know it
knows. If I could make you and Austin proud
someday, a long way off, 'twould give me taller
feet.

EMILY

She never told her family of her writing, and this is
the only mention of any secret ambition to have her
work known even on a day 'a long way off.' The first
poem dated, that she sent to Sister Sue, was in 1848,
and probably the last word she ever wrote was her reply
to a message from her—

My answer is an unmitigated *Yes*, Sue.

EMILY

McNally Editions reissues books that are not widely known but have stood the test of time, that remain as singular and engaging as when they were written. Available in the US wherever books are sold or by subscription from mcnallyeditions.com.